Spurgeon's Sermons
on
New Testament Men

Book One

C. H. Spurgeon Resources

A Classic Bible Study Library for Today
Commenting and Commentaries
Day by Day with C. H. Spurgeon (compiled by Al Bryant)
The Treasury of David (edited by David Otis Fuller)
Spurgeon's Sermon Illustrations
Spurgeon's Sermon Notes
Spurgeon's Sermons on the Cross of Christ
Spurgeon's Sermons on Old Testament Men • Book One
Spurgeon's Sermons on Old Testament Women • Book One
Spurgeon's Sermons on Prayer
Spurgeon's Sermons on the Resurrection of Christ
Spurgeon's Sermons on Soulwinning

Spurgeon's Sermons on New Testament Men

Book One

CHARLES HADDON SPURGEON

kregel
PUBLICATIONS

Grand Rapids, MI 49501

Spurgeon's Sermons on New Testament Men • *Book One*
by Charles H. Spurgeon.

Copyright © 1994 by Kregel Publications.

Published by Kregel Publications, a division of Kregel, Inc.,
P.O. Box 2607, Grand Rapids, MI 49501. Kregel
Publications provides trusted, biblical publications for
Christian growth and service. Your comments and sug-
gestions are valued.

Cover artwork: Don Ellens
Cover and book design: Alan G. Hartman

Library of Congress Cataloging-in-Publication Data

Spurgeon, C. H. (Charles Haddon), 1834–1892.
   [Sermons on New Testament men]
   Spurgeon's Sermons on New Testament Men • Book
One / by Charles H. Spurgeon.
     p.   cm.
   1. Men in the Bible—Biography—Sermons. 2. Bible.
N.T.—Biography—Sermons. 3. Sermons, English.
4. Baptists—Sermons. I. Title. II. Series: Spurgeon,
C. H. (Charles Haddon), 1834–1892. C. H. Spurgeon
sermon series.
BS2447.S78   1994   220.9'2'081—dc20   94-13039
                                            CIP
ISBN 0-8254-3783-0 (pbk.)

1 2 3 4 5 printing / year 98 97 96 95 94

Contents

"Analyze the gifts of that powerful evangelist as accurately as you can; measure, as closely as may be possible, the secret of his influence; but I do not believe that you will find any other teacher whose printed sermons would be read week after week, year after year, by tens and hundreds of thousands, not only all over England, Scotland, and Wales, but in the backwoods of Canada, on the prairies of America, in the remotest settlements of Australia and New Zealand, wherever an English newspaper can reach, or the English tongue is spoken. The thing is absolutely unique. It has no parallel. . . . What was it that gave [Spurgeon] a religious influence so unparalleled in our day, and made his name a household word all over the wide world? No doubt he had rare gifts. He was courageous, resolute, and lively in these times of the faint heart, irresolution and dullness. He had that genuine eloquence which is all the more effective because of its directness and simplicity. He had a matchless voice, powerful and vibrating with every quality of earnestness and variety. He had humor, tender pathos, and never failed to be interesting. He was utterly untrammelled by the questionings of criticism. But it was, above all, the splendid completeness, the unswerving strength, the exuberant vitality of his faith in God's revelation to man through His Son Jesus Christ, combined with the width and warmth of his zealous love for souls, that gave him that unbounded power which he exercised so loyally for Christian belief. . . ."

Archdeacon Sinclair of St. Paul's Cathedral
on the impact of Spurgeon's ministry

1

*Loosing the Shoe-Latchet**

*One mightier than I cometh, the latchet of whose shoes I am not
worthy to unloose (Luke 3:16).*

It was not John's business to attract followers to himself but to point
them to Jesus, and he very faithfully discharged his commission. His
opinion of his Master, of whom he was the herald, was a very high one;
he reverenced Him as the anointed of the Lord, the King of Israel, and,
consequently, he was not tempted into elevating himself into a rival. He
rejoiced to declare "he must increase but I must decrease." In the course
of his self-depreciation, he uses the expression of our text, which is recorded by each one of the evangelists, with some little variation. Matthew
words it, "whose shoes I am not worthy to bear"; he was not fit to fetch his
Lord His shoes. Mark writes it "whose shoes I am not worthy to stoop
down and unloose"; and John has it very much as in Luke. This putting on,
and taking off and putting away of sandals, was an office usually left to
menial servants, it was not a work of any repute or honor, yet the Baptist
felt that it would be a great honor to be even a menial servant of the Lord
Jesus. He felt that the Son of God was so infinitely superior to himself that
he was honored if only permitted to be the meanest slave in His employ.
He would not allow men to attempt comparisons between himself and
Jesus, he felt that none could, for a moment, be allowed. Now this honest
estimate of himself as less than nothing in comparison with his Master is
greatly to be imitated by us. John is to be commended and admired for this,
but better still he is to be carefully copied.

Remember that John was by no means an inferior man. Among all that
had been born of women before his time there had not been a greater than
he. He was the subject of many prophecies, and his office was a peculiarly
noble one; he was the friend of the great Bridegroom, and introduced Him

---

* This sermon is taken from *The Metropolitan Tabernacle Pulpit* and was
preached on Sunday morning, March 31, 1872.

9

to His chosen bride. He was the morning star of the gospel day, but he counted himself no light in the presence of the Sun of Righteousness whom he heralded. The temperament of John was not that which bowed or cringed; he was no reed shaken by the wind, no man of courtly habits fitted for king's palace. No. We see in him in Elias, a man of iron, a son of thunder; he roared like a young lion on his prey, and feared the face of none. Some men are so naturally meek spirited, not to say weak-minded, that they naturally become subservient and set up others as their leaders, such men are apt to err in depreciating themselves; but John was every inch a man, his great soul bowed only before that which was worthy of homage; he was in God's strength as an iron pillar and a brazen wall, a hero for the cause of the Lord, and yet he sat down in the presence of Jesus as a little child at school sits at his master's feet, and he cried "whose shoe-latchet I am not worthy to stoop down and to unloose."

Recollect, moreover, that John was a man endowed with great abilities, and these are very apt to make a man proud. He was a prophet, yea, and more than a prophet. When he stood in the wilderness to preach, his burning eloquence soon attracted the people from Jerusalem and from all the cities round about, and the banks of Jordan saw a vast multitude of eager hearers crowding around the man clothed with a garment of camel's hair. Thousands gathered together to listen to the teaching of one who had not been brought up at the feet of the rabbis, neither had been taught eloquence after the fashion of the schools. John was a man of bold, plain, telling, commanding speech; he was no second-rate teacher, but a master in Israel, yet he assumed no airs of self-conceit, but accounted the lowest place in the Lord's service as too high for him. Note, too, that he was not only a great preacher, but he had been very successful not only in attracting the crowds but in baptizing them. The whole nation felt the effects of John's ministry, and knew that he was a prophet: they were swayed to and fro by his zealous words, as the corn of autumn is moved in the breath of the wind. A man is very apt when he feels that he has power over masses of his fellow creatures to be lifted up and exalted above measure, but not so John. It was safe for the Lord to trust him with a great popularity and a great success, for though he had all those honors he laid them meekly down at Jesus' feet, and said, "I am not worthy to be even the lowest slave in Messiah's household."

Reflect, also, moreover, that John was a religious leader, and he had the opportunity, if he had pleased, of becoming the leader of a powerful sect. The people were evidently willing to follow him. There were some, no doubt, who would not have gone over to Christ himself if John had not bidden them go, and testified, "Behold the Lamb of God," and confessed over and over again, saying, "I am not the Christ." We read of some who years after the Baptist was dead still remained his disciples, so that he had the opportunity of leading away a multitude who would have become his followers, and so of setting up his own name among men; but he scorned it, his elevated view of his master prevented his entertaining any desire for personal leadership, and putting himself down not in the place of a captain of the Lord's hosts, but as one of the least soldiers in the army, he said, "His shoe latchets I am not worthy to unloose." What was the reason, think you, of John's always retaining his proper position? Was it not because he had a high idea of his Master, and a deep reverence for Him? Ah, brethren, because of our little estimate of Christ, it is often unsafe for the Lord to trust us in any but the very lowest positions. I believe many of us might have been ten times as useful, only it would not have been safe for God to have allowed us to be so; we should have been puffed up, and like Nebuchadnezzar we should have boasted, "Behold this great Babylon that I have builded." Many a man has had to fight in the back ranks, and serve his Master but little, and enjoy but little success in that service, because he did not reverence Christ enough, did not love his Lord enough, and, consequently, self would soon have crept in to his own overturning, to the grief of the church, and to the dishonor of his Lord. Oh, for high thoughts of Christ, and low thoughts of ourselves! Oh, to see Jesus as filling all in all, and to be ourselves as less than nothing before Him.

Having thus introduced the subject, our object this morning is to draw instruction from the expression which John here and elsewhere used with regard to himself and his Lord: "Whose shoe-latchet I am not worthy to unloose."

I gather from this, first, that *no form of holy service is to be lightly set by*: secondly, that *our unworthiness is apparent in the presence of any sort of holy work*: but that, thirdly, *this unworthiness of ours, when most felt, should rather stimulate us to action than discourage us*, for so it doubtless operated in the case of John the Baptist.

No Form of Holy Service Is to Be Lightly Set By

First, then, note that NO FORM OF HOLY SERVICE IS TO BE LIGHTLY SET BY. To unloose the latchets of Christ's shoes might seem very trivial; it might even seem as if it involved the loss of self-respect for a man of position and influence to stoop to offices which a servant might quite as well perform. Why should I bring myself down to that? I will learn of Christ; I will distribute bread among the multitude for Christ; I will have my boat by the sea shore ready for Christ to preach in, or I will go and fetch the ass upon which He shall ride in triumph into Jerusalem: but what need can there be for the disciple to become a mere menial? Such a question as that is here forever silenced, and the spirit which dictates it is practically rebuked. Nothing is dishonorable by which Jesus may be honored. Nothing lowers a man if thereby he honors his Lord. It is not possible for any godly work to be beneath our dignity; rather ought we to know that the lowest grade of service bestows dignity upon the man who heartily performs it. Even the least and most obscure form of serving Christ is more high and lofty than we are worthy to undertake.

Now, note that little works for Christ, little shoe bearings and latchet loosings, often *have more of the child's spirit in them than greater works.* Outside, in the streets, a man's companion will do him a kindness, and the action performed is friendly; but for filial acts you must look inside the house. There the child does not lend money to his father, or negotiate business, yet in his little acts there is more sonship. Who is it that comes to meet father when the day is over? And what is the action which often indicates childhood's love? See the little child comes tottering forward with father's slippers, and runs off with his boots as he puts them off. The service is little, but it is loving and filial, and has more of filial affection in it than the servant's bringing in the meal, of preparing the bed, or any other more essential service. It gives the little one great pleasure, and expresses his love. No one who is not my child, or who does not love me in something like the same way, would ever dream of making such a service his specialty. The littleness of the act fits it to the child's capacity, and there is also something in it which makes it a suitable expression of a child's affection. So also in little acts for Jesus. Oftentimes men of the world will give their money to the cause of Christ, putting down large sums for charity or for missions, but they will not weep in secret over other men's sins, or speak a word of comfort to an afflicted saint. To visit a poor sick woman, teach a little child, reclaim a street Arab, breathe a prayer for enemies, or whisper a promise in the ear of a desponding saint, may show more of sonship than building a row of almshouses or endowing a church.

In little acts for Christ it is always to be remembered that the *little things are as necessary to be done as the greater acts.* If Christ's feet be not washed, if His sandals be not unloosed He may suffer, and His feet may be lamed, so that a journey may be shortened, and many villages may miss the blessing of His presence. So with other minor things. There is as much need for the quiet intercessions of saints as for the public delivery of God's truth before the assembled thousands. It is as needful that babes be taught their little hymns as that monarchs be rebuked for sin. We remember the old story of the losing of the battle through the missing of a single nail in a horse-shoe, and peradventure up to this moment the church may have lost her battle for Christ, because some minor work which ought to have been done for Jesus has been neglected. I should not wonder if it should turn out that many churches have been without prosperity because, while they have looked to the public ministry and the visible ordinances, they have been negligent of smaller usefulnesses. Many a cart comes to grief through inattention to the linchpin. A very small matter turns an arrow aside from the target. To teach a child to sing "Gentle Jesus," and to point his young heart to the Redeemer, may seem a trifle, but yet it may be a most essential part of the process of that gracious work of religious education by which that child shall afterward become a believer, a minister, and a winner of souls. Omit that first lesson and it may be you have turned aside a life. Take another instance. A preacher once found himself advertised to preach in an obscure village, the storm was terrible, and, therefore, though he kept his appointment, he found only one person present in the place of meeting. He preached a sermon to that one hearer with as much earnestness as if the house had been crowded. Years after he found churches all over the district, and he discovered that his audience of one had been converted on that day, and had become the evangelist of the whole region. Had he declined to preach to one, what blessings might have been withheld. Brethren, never neglect the loosing of the shoe-latchet for Christ, since you do not know what may hang upon it. Human destiny often turns upon a hinge so small as to be invisible. Never say within yourself, "This is trivial"—nothing is trivial for the Lord. Never say, "But this surely might be omitted without much loss." How do you know? If it be your duty, He who allotted you the task knew what he did. Do not in any measure neglect any portion of His orders, for in all His commands there is consummate wisdom, and on your part it will be wisdom to obey them, even to the jots and tittles.

Little things for Christ again are *often the best tests of the truth of our religion*. Obedience in little things has much to do with the character of a servant. You engage a servant in your own house, and you know very well whether she be a good or bad servant that the main duties of the day are pretty sure to be attended to; the meals will be cooked, the beds will be prepared, the house will be swept, the door will be answered; but the difference between a servant who makes the house happy and another who is its plague, lies in a number of small matters, which, peradventure, you could not put down on paper, but which make up a very great deal of domestic comfort or discomfort, and so determine the value of a servant. So I believe it is in Christian life; I do not suppose that the most of us here would ever omit the weightier matters of the law; as Christian men we endeavor to maintain integrity and uprightness in our actions, and we try to order our households in the fear of God in great matters; but it is in the looking to the Lord upon minor details that the spirit of obedience is most displayed; it is seen in our keeping our eye up to the Lord, as the eyes of the handmaidens are to their mistresses for daily orders about this step and that transaction. The really obedient spirit wishes to know the Lord's will about everything, and if there be any point which to the world seem trifling, for that very reason the obedient spirit says, "I will attend to it to prove to my Lord that even in the minute things I desire to submit my soul to His good pleasure." In small things lie the crucibles and the touchstones. Any hypocrite will come to the Sabbath worship, but it is not every hypocrite that will attend prayer meetings, or read the Bible in secret, or speak privately of the things of God to the saints. These are less things, so they judge, and therefore they neglect them, and so condemn themselves. Where there is deep religion prayer is loved: where religion is shallow only public acts of worship are called for. You shall find the same true in other things. A man who is no Christian will very likely not tell you a downright lie by saying that black is white, but he will not hesitate to declare that whitybrown is white—he will go that length. Now, the Christian will not go halfway to falsehood, nay, he scorns to go an inch on that road. He will no more cheat you out of twopence farthing, than he would out of two thousand pounds. He will not rob you of an inch any more than of an ell. It is in the little that the genuineness of the Christian is made to appear; the Goldsmiths' Hall mark is a small affair, but you know true silver by it. There is a vast deal of difference between the man who gladly bears Christ's shoes, and another who will not stoop to anything which he thinks beneath him. Even a Pharisee will ask Christ to his house to sit at meat with him, he is willing to entertain a great religious leader at his table; but it is not everyone who will stoop down and unloose His shoes, for that very Pharisee who made the feast neither brought Him water to wash His feet, nor gave Him the kiss of welcome. He proved the insincerity of his hospitality by forgetting the little things. I will be bound to say Martha and Mary never forgot to unloose His shoe-latchets, and that Lazarus never failed to see that His feet were washed. Look then, I pray you, as Christians to the service of Christ in the obscure things, in the things that are not recognized by men, in the matters which have no honor attached to them, for by this shall your love be tried.

Mark, also, with regard to little works that very often *there is about them a degree of personal fellowship with Christ which is not seen in greater work.* For instance, in the one before us, to unloose the latchets of His shoes brings me into contact with Himself, though it be only His feet I touch; and I think if I might have the preference between going forth to cast out devils and to preach the gospel and to heal the sick, or to stay with Him and always loose the latchets of His shoes, I should prefer this last; because the first act Judas did—he went with the twelve and saw Satan like lightning fall from heaven, but he perished because he failed in the acts that came into contact with Christ—in keeping Christ's purse he was a thief, and in giving Christ the kiss he was a traitor. He who does not fail in things relating personally to Christ is the sound man, he has the evidence of righteousness of heart. There was never a grander action done beneath the stars than when the woman broke her alabaster box of precious ointment and poured it upon Him; though the poor did not get anything out of it, though no sick man was the better for it, the act was done distinctly unto Him, and therefore there was a peculiar sweetness in it. Oftentimes similar actions, because they do not encourage other people for they do not know of them, because they may not be of any very great value to our fellow men, are lightly esteemed, yet seeing they are done for Christ, they have about them a peculiar charm as terminating upon His blessed person. True, it is but the loosing of shoe-latchets, but then, they are His shoes, and that ennobles the deed.

Dear fellow Christians, you know what I mean, though I cannot put it into very good language this morning—I mean just this, that if there is some little thing I can do for Christ, though my minister will not know about it, though the deacons and elders will not know, and nobody will know, and if I leave it undone nobody will suffer any calamity because of it; but, if I do it, it will please my Lord, and I shall enjoy the sense of having done it to Him, therefore will I attend to it, for it is no slight work if it be *for Him.*

Mark, also, once more, concerning those gracious actions which are but little esteemed by the most of mankind, that we know *God accepts our worship in little things.* He allowed His people to bring their bullocks, others of them to bring their rams, and offer them to Him; and these were persons of sufficient wealth to be able to afford a tribute from their herds and flocks, but He also permitted the poor to offer a pair of turtle doves, or two young pigeons, and I have never found in God's Word that He cared less for the turtle dove offering than He did for the sacrifice of the bullock. I do know, too, that our ever blessed Lord himself, when He was here, loved the praise of little children. They brought neither gold nor silver like the wise men from the East, but they cried "Hosanna," and the Lord was not angry with their Hosannas, but accepted their boyish praise. And we remember that a widow woman cast into the treasury two mites, which only made a farthing, but, because it was all her living, He did not reject the gift, but rather recorded it to her honor. We are now quite familiar with the incident, but for all that it is very wonderful. Two mites that make a farthing given to the infinite God! A farthing accepted by the King of kings! A farthing acknowledged by Him who made the heavens and the earth, who said, "If I were hungry I would not tell thee, for the cattle on a thousand hills are mine." Two mites received with pleasure by the Lord of all! It was scarcely so much as a drop thrown into the sea, and yet he thought much of it. Measure, therefore, not little actions by human scales and measures, but estimate them as God does, for the Lord has respect unto the hearts of His people; He regards not so much their deeds in themselves as the motives by which they are actuated. Therefore, value the loosing of the Savior's shoe-latchets, and despise not the day of small things.

Our Own Unworthiness

Now, brethren and sisters, I wish to conduct you, in the second place, to the consideration of OUR OWN UNWORTHINESS, which is sure to be felt by us whenever we come practically into contact with any real Christian service. I believe that a man who does nothing at all thinks himself a fine fellow, as a general rule. You shall usually find that the sharpest critics are those who never write; and the best judges of battles those who keep at a prudent distance from the guns. Christians of the kid-gloved order, who never make an attempt to save souls, are marvelously quick to tell us when we are too rough or too light in our speech; and they readily detect us if our modes of action are irregular or too enthusiastic. They have a very keen scent for anything like fanaticism or disorder. For my part, I feel pretty safe when I have the censures of these gentlemen; we are not far wrong when they condemn us. Let a man begin earnestly to work for the Lord Jesus, and he will soon find out that he is unworthy of the meanest place in the employ of One so glorious. Let us turn over that fact a minute. Dear brothers and sisters, when we *recollect what we used to be* I am sure we must feel unworthy to do the very least thing for Christ. You know how Paul describes the wickedness of certain offenders, and he adds, "But such were some of you." What hardness of heart some of us exhibited toward God! what rebellion! what obstinacy! what quenching of His Spirit! what love of sin! Why, if I might stoop down to unloose the latchet of the shoe of that foot which was crucified for me, I must bedew the nail print with my tears, and say, "My Savior, can it be that I am ever allowed to touch Your feet?" Surely, the prodigal, if he ever unloosed his father's shoes, would say to himself, "Why, these hands fed the swine, these hands were often polluted by the harlots, I lived in uncleanness, and was first a reveler, and then a swineherd, and it is amazing love which permits me now to serve so good a father." Angels in heaven might envy the man who is permitted to do the least thing for Christ, and yet they never sinned. Oh, what a favor that we who are defiled with sin should be called to serve the sinless Savior.

But, then, another reflection comes at the back of it—*we recollect what we are* as well as what we were—I say, what we are, for though washed in Jesus' blood, and endowed with a new heart and a right spirit, yet we start aside like a deceitful bow, for corruption dwells in us. It is sometimes hard work to maintain even a little faith, we are so double-minded, so unstable, so hot, so cold, so earnest, and then so negligent: we are so everything except what we ought to be, that we may well wonder that Christ allows us to do the least thing for Him. If He were to shut us in prison and keep us there, so long as He did not actually execute us, He would be dealing with us according to mercy, and not giving us our full deserts and yet He calls us out of prison, and puts us in His service, and therefore we feel that we are unworthy to perform the least action in His house.

Besides, beloved, even *small services we feel require a better state of heart than we often have.* I am sure the service of preaching the gospel here often brings to my sight my unworthiness far more than I should otherwise see it. If it be a gracious thing to see one's sinfulness, I may thank God I preach the gospel, for it makes me see it. Sometimes we come to preach about Jesus Christ and glorify Him, and yet our heart is not warm toward Him, and we do not value Him aright; while the text we are preaching from seats Him on a high throne, our heart is not setting Him there; and oh, then we think we could tear our heart out of our very body, if we could get rid of the black drops of its depravity which prevent our feeling in unison with the glorious truth before us. Another time, perhaps, we have to invite sinners and seek to bring them to Christ, and that wants so much sympathy that if Christ were preaching our sermon He would bedew it with His tears; but, we deliver it with dry eyes, almost without emotion, and then we flog our hard heart that it will not stir and cannot be made to feel. It is just the same in other duties. Have you not felt "I have to go and teach my class, this afternoon, but I am not fit, I have been worried all the week with cares, and my mind is not up to the mark now; I hope I love my Lord, but I hardly know whether I do or not. I ought to be earnest about these boys and girls: but it is very likely I shall not be earnest, I shall sit down and go through my teaching as a parrot would go through it, without life, without love." Yes, then you painfully feel that you are not worthy to unloose the latchets of your Lord's shoes. Possibly, you are going this afternoon to visit a dying man, and you will try and talk to him about the way to heaven. He is unconverted. Now, you want a tongue of fire to speak with, and instead of that, you have a tongue of ice: you feel, "God, how can it be that I shall sit by that bedside and think of that poor man, who will be in the flames of hell, perhaps, within a week, unless he receive Christ, and yet I shall coolly treat his tremendously perilous condition as though it were a matter of the very slightest consequence." Yes, yes, yes, we have had hundred of times to feel that we are in end of ourselves not fit for anything. If the Lord wanted scullions in His kitchen, He could get better than we are; and if He needed someone to shovel out the refuse of His house He could find better men than we are for that. To such a Master we are unworthy to be servants.

The same feeling arises in another way. Have we not to confess, brethren and sisters, in looking upon what we have done for Christ, that *we have far too much eye to self in our conduct.* We pick and choose our work, and the picking and choosing is guided by the instinct of self-respect. If we are asked to do that which is pleasant to ourselves we do it. If we are requested to attend a meeting where we shall be received with acclamation, if we are asked to perform a service which will lift us up in the social scale, or that will commend us to our fellow Christians, we jump at it like a fish at a fly; but, suppose the work would bring us shame, suppose it would discover to the public rather our inefficiency than our ability, we excuse ourselves. The spirit which Moses felt a little of, when the Lord called him, is upon many of us. "If I were to speak for Christ," says one, "I should stutter and stammer." As if God did not make stuttering mouths as well as fluent mouths; and as if, when He chose a Moses, He did not know what He was at. Moses must go and stammer for God, and glorify God by stammering, but Moses does not like that; and many in similar cases have not had grace enough to go to the work at all. Why, if I cannot honor the Lord with ten talents, shall I refuse to serve Him with one? If I cannot fly like a strong-winged angel through the midst of heaven, and sound the shrill-mouthed trumpet so as to wake the dead, shall I refuse to be a little bee and gather honey at God's bidding? Because I cannot be a leviathan, shall I refuse to be an ant? What folly and what rebellion if we are so perverse.

And, if you have performed any holy work, have you not noticed that pride is ready to rise? God can hardly let us succeed in any work but what we become toplofty. "Oh, how well we have done it!" We do not want anybody to say, "Now, that was very cleverly, and nicely, and carefully, and earnestly done," for we say all that to ourselves, and we add, "yes, you were zealous about that work, and you have been doing what a great many would not have done, and you have not boasted of it either. You do not call in any neighbor to see it, you have been doing it simply out of love to God, and, therefore you are an uncommonly humble fellow, and none can say you are vain." Alas! what flattery, but truly "the heart is deceitful above all things, and desperately wicked." We are not worthy to unloose the latchets of Jesus' shoes, because, if we do, we begin to say to ourselves, "What great folks are we; we have been allowed to loose the latchets of the Lord's sandals." If we do not tell somebody else about it with many an exultation, we at least tell ourselves about it, and feel that we are something after all, and ought to be held in no small repute.

My brethren, we ought to feel that we are not worthy to do the lowest thing we can do for Christ, because, *when we have gone to the lowest, Jesus always goes lower down than we have gone.* Is it a little thing to bear His shoes? What, then, was His condescension when He washed His disciples' feet? To put up with a cross-tempered brother, to be gentle with him, and feel, "I will give way to him in everything because I am a Christian," that is going very low; but then, our Lord has borne far more from us; He was patient with His people's infirmities, and forgave even to seventy times seven. And, suppose we are willing to take the lowest place in the church, yet Jesus took a lower place than we can, for He took the place of the curse—He was made sin for us, even He that knew no sin, that we might be made the righteousness of God in Him. I have sometimes felt willing to go to the gates of hell to save a soul; but the Redeemer went further, for He suffered the wrath of God for souls. If there should be any Christian here who is so humble that he has no lofty thoughts about himself, but prefers to be least among his brethren, and so proves his graciousness, yet, my dear brother, you are not so lowly as Christ made Himself, for he "made himself of no reputation," and you love some reputation left; and He took upon Himself the form of a servant, and he became obedient to death, you have not come to that yet; even the death of the cross—the felon's death upon the gibbet, you will never be brought to that. Oh, the stoop of the Redeemer's amazing love! Let us, henceforth, contend how low we can go side by side with him, but remember when we have gone to the lowest He descends lower still, so that we can truly feel that the very lowest place is too high for us, because He has gone lower still.

Beloved friends, to put these things in a practical shape, it may seem to be a very small duty for any of you to do, to speak to one person alone about his soul. If you were asked to preach to a hundred you would try it. I ask you solemnly, in God's name, not to let the sun go down today till you have spoken to one man or woman alone about his or her soul. Will you not do that? Is it too little for you? Then I must be plain with you, and say you are not worthy to do it. Speak today to some little child about his soul. Do not say, "Oh, we cannot talk to children, we cannot stoop to them." Let no such feeling occupy any of our minds, for if this work be as the loosing of the Master's shoe-latchets, let us do it. Holy Brainerd, when he was dying, and could no longer preach to the Indians, had a little Indian boy at his bedside, and taught him his letters; and he remarked to one who came in, "I asked God that I might not live any longer than I could be of use, and so, as I cannot preach any more, I am teaching this poor little child to read the Bible." Let us never think that we are stooping when we teach children, but if it be stooping let us stoop.

There are some of you, perhaps, who have the opportunity to do good to fallen women. Do you shrink from such work? Many do. They feel as if they could do anything rather than speak to such. Is it the loosing of the latchet of your Master's shoe? It is, then, an honorable business; try it, brother. It is not beneath you if you do it for Jesus; it is even above the best of you, you are not worthy to do it. Possibly there is near your house a district of very poor people. You do not like going in among them. They are dirty, and perhaps infected with disease. Well, it is a pity that poor people should so often be dirty, but pride is dirty too. Do you say, "I cannot go there." Why not? Are you such a mighty fine gentleman that you are afraid of soiling your hands? You will not unloose your Master's shoe-latchet then. The Lord lived among the poor, and was poorer even than they; for He had not where to lay His head. Oh, shame on you, you wicked and proud servant of a condescending, loving Lord! Go about your business, and unloose the latchets of His shoes directly! Instead of imagining that you would be lowered by such work for Jesus, I tell you it would honor you; indeed, you are not fit for it, the honor is too great for you, and will fall to the lot of better men.

It comes to this, beloved, anything that can be done for Christ is too good for us to do. Somebody wanted to keep the door! Somebody wanted to rout out the back lanes! Somebody wanted to teach ragged roughs! Somebody wanted to ask people to come to the place of worship, and to lend them their seats, and stand in the aisle while they sit. Well, be it what it may, I had rather be a door keeper in the house of the Lord, or the door mat either, than I would be accounted among the noblest in the tents of wickedness. Anything for Jesus, the lower the better; anything for Jesus, the humbler the better; anything for Jesus. The more going down into the deeps, the more thrusting the arms up to the elbows in the mud to find out precious jewels, the more of that the better. This is the true spirit of the Christian religion. Not the soaring up there to sit among the choristers, and sing in grand style, not the putting on of apparel, and preaching in lawn sleeves; not the going through gaudy and imposing ceremonies—all that is of Babylon: but to strip yourself to the shirt sleeves to fight the battle for Christ, and to go out among men as a humble worker, resolved by any means to save some, this is what your Lord would have you to do, for this is the unloosing of the latchets of His shoes.

All This Ought to Stimulate Us and Not Discourage Us

And, now, our last remark shall be that ALL THIS OUGHT TO STIMULATE US AND NOT DISCOURAGE US. Though we are not worthy to do it, that is the reason why we should avail ourselves of the condescending grace which honors us with such employ. Do not say, "I am not worthy to unloose the latchets of His shoes, and, therefore, I shall give up preaching." Oh no, but preach away with all the greater vigor. John did so, and to his preaching he added warning. Warn people as well as preach to them. Tell them of the judgment to come, and separate between the precious and the vile. We should perform our work in all ways, not omitting the more painful part of it, but going through with whatever God has appointed to us. John was called to testify of Christ, he felt unworthy to do it, but he did not shirk the work. It was his lifelong business to cry, "Behold, behold, behold the Lamb of God!" and he did it earnestly; he never paused in that cry. He was busy in baptizing too. It was the initiatory rite of the new dispensation, and there he stood continually immersing those who believed. Never a more indefatigable worker than John the Baptist; he threw his whole soul into it, because he felt he was not worthy to do the work. Brethren and sisters, your sense of unworthiness will, if you be idle, sadly hamper you; but if the love of God be in your soul you will feel, "Since I do so badly when I do my best, I will always do my utmost. Since it comes to so little when the most is done, I will at least do the most." Could I give all my substance to Him, and give my life, and then give my body to be burned, it would be a small return for love so amazing, so divine, as that which I have tasted: therefore, if I cannot do all that, at any rate, I will give the Lord Jesus all

I can, I will love Him all I can, I will pray to Him all I can, I will talk about Him all I can, and I will spread His gospel all I can; and no little thing will I count beneath me if His cause require it.

Brethren, John lived hard, for his meat was locusts and wild honey; his dress was not the soft raiment of men who live in palaces, he wrapped about him the rough camel's skin; and as he lived hard he died hard too, his boldness brought him into a dungeon, his courageous fidelity earned him a martyr's death. Here was a man who lived in self-denial and died witnessing for truth and righteousness, and all this because he had a high esteem of his Master. May our esteem of Christ so grow and increase that we may be willing to put up with anything in life for Christ, and even to lay down our lives for His name's sake!

Certain Moravian missionaries, in the old times of slavery, went to one of the West Indian Islands to preach, and they found they could not be permitted to teach there unless they themselves became slaves; and they did so, they sold themselves into bondage, never to return, that they might save slaves' souls. We have heard of another pair of holy men who actually submitted to be confined in a lazar-house that they might save the souls of lepers, knowing as they did that they would never be permitted to come out again; they went there to take the leprosy and to die, if by so doing they might save souls. I have read of one, Thomé de Jesu, who went to Barbary amongst the Christian captives, and there lived and died in banishment and bondage, that he might cheer his brethren, and preach Jesus to them. Brethren, we have never reached to such devotion; we fall far short of what Jesus deserves. We give Him little, we give Him what we are ashamed not to give Him. Often we give Him our zeal for a day or two and then grow cool, we wake up on a sudden and then sleep all the more soundly. We seem today as if we would set the world on fire, and tomorrow we scarce keep our own lamp trimmed. We vow at one time that we will push the church before us and drag the world after us, and by-and-by we ourselves are like Pharaoh's chariots with the wheels taken off, and drag along right heavily. Oh, for a spark of the love of Christ in the soul! Oh, for a living flame from off Calvary's altar, to set our whole nature blazing with divine enthusiasm for the Christ who gave Himself for us that we might live! Henceforth, take upon yourselves in the solemn intent of your soul this deep resolve: "I will unloose the latchets of His shoes, I will seek out the little things, the mean things, the humble things, and I will do them as unto the Lord and not unto men, and may He accept me even as He has saved me through His precious blood." Amen.

2

The Far-Off, Near;
The Near, Far Off*

Now when Jesus was born in Bethlehem of Judea in the days of Herod the king, behold, there came wise men from the east to Jerusalem, saying, Where is he that is born King of the Jews? for we have seen his star in the east, and are come to worship him. When Herod the king had heard these things, he was troubled, and all Jerusalem with him. And when he had gathered all the chief priests and scribes of the people together, he demanded of them where Christ should be born (Matthew 2:1–4).

I am not going to expound the whole passage that I have read as a text; but I desire to help you to gather some lessons from this familiar narrative.

"When Jesus was born." A stir begins as soon as Christ is born. He has not spoken a word; He has not wrought a miracle; He has not proclaimed a single doctrine; but "when Jesus was born," at the very first, while as yet you hear nothing but infant cries, and can see nothing but infant weakness, still His influence upon the world is manifest. "When Jesus was born, there came wise men from the east," and so on. There is infinite power even in an infant Savior. When Jesus is born in the heart, and there are only the feeblest impulses toward righteousness and repentance with regard to sin, He makes a stir in our whole nature. The most distant faculty feels that something wonderful has happened. When Christ is formed in us, the hope of glory, a sacred revolution commences within us. When Christ is born in a village, a town, a city, the first sinner converted, the first open-air sermon preached, the first giving away of sacred literature, makes a stir. It is wonderful how soon it begins to manifest itself. Somebody or other is affected

---

* This sermon is taken from *The Metropolitan Tabernacle Pulpit* and was preached on Sunday evening, August 11, 1889.

by the fact that Christ has come; He cannot be hid. The first match struck makes a great blaze. Jesus of Nazareth is so potent a factor in the world of mind that, no sooner is He there in His utmost weakness, a newborn King, than He begins to reign. Before He mounts the throne, friends bring Him presents, and His enemies compass His death. Oh, that the Lord Jesus might be here tonight, if it be but as new born, in some few hearts! There will be a result from Christ's coming, even though I preach Him very feebly, though you may say that I can only bring to you an infant Christ, though my power of speech may fail me, and I may but set Him forth in His littleness rather than in His greatness. When Christ is born, when Christ is only feebly preached, when Christ is but stammered out, a great result comes of it, and His name is made glorious.

There were two results from Christ's coming, as there always will be, for this Child is not only a Savior to some, but also a stumbling-block to others. His gospel is either "a savor of life unto life," or else "a savor of death unto death." I want you, first, to notice the note of exclamation that we have in the first verse. "When Jesus was born, *behold.*" *Ecce!* Behold! There is something to look at, something good that is worth gazing upon. Behold it. *Here are far-off persons who come very nigh.* Wise men come and worship the infant Christ; but there is something to which there is no "behold" put, yet it is sorrowfully worth considering. *Here are near ones who are far off,* Herod, the inhabitants of Jerusalem, the chief priests, and the scribes. They are as far from Christ as if He had been born in the distant east, while they who lived in the far country came as near to Him as if they themselves had dwelt at Bethlehem. So I have these two things to talk about tonight, first, the extraordinary fact that many far-off ones are brought nigh, and the sad but almost equally extraordinary fact that many who are apparently very near never really come nigh to Jesus.

There Are Far-Off Ones Brought Nigh

To begin, then, at the beginning. THERE ARE FAR-OFF ONES BROUGHT NIGH. God saves whom He wills to save; His grace is most sovereign. You cannot see, as I do, so many persons brought to Christ without often wondering why they were brought. I have often seen the last first, and the first last; people of whose conversion I should hardly have dreamed become converted, while other persons, for whom I have hoped, and over whom I have prayed, remain unconverted. It is very delightful, as well as very wonderful, to notice the strange way in which the grace of God singles out individuals, and the marvelous measures which the God of grace uses to bring these individuals to the feet of Jesus.

Well now, first, these people were *wise men*, magi, students of astronomy, learned in the lore of the ancients. Their philosophy was not a very true one; it was about as true as modern philosophy, which is not saying much. They believed very absurd things, these magi, almost as absurd as the scientists of the present day, perhaps not quite as ridiculous, for science has grown in absurdity, especially of late; but these men were professors of the philosophy of the period. They were the wise men. If they came from Media, they were probably fire-worshipers, or worshipers of the elements of nature. Theirs was a refined form of idolatry, which is not to be excused; but still, if there can be any choice where all is bad, it is perhaps a little hotter than some others. They were very great students so far as their light went; they sought after knowledge and wisdom. Well now, truth to tell, it is not many of this sort of people who come to Christ. His doctrine is too simple for them; He himself lays the ax too near the root of the tree; His teaching is too plain. They are so wise that His wisdom baffles them. They know so much, as they think; yet His better and higher knowledge overshadows theirs, and they cannot brook it, and yield to Him. "Not many wise men after the flesh, not many mighty, not many noble, are called"; but here the infinite sovereignty of God calls these wise men first; no, I must not say first, for the shepherds came first; but next to the shepherds, the Lord calls those wise men from the distant east. It has been truly remarked that the shepherds did not miss their way; they came to Christ at once, while the wise men, even with a star to guide them, yet missed their way, and went to Jerusalem instead of Bethlehem, and inquired at the palace of Herod, instead of at the stable where the Christ was born. However, they did come to Christ, even if they did come in a roundabout way, and make a blunder or two. Here was the wonder, that they did come; and if I address myself tonight, as I would do most respectfully; to any here who excel in human wisdom, how I wish they would join divinity to their humanities; and if they know much, yet I long that, with all their knowledge they would know Christ, and with all their gettings that they would get understanding; for the science of Christ crucified is the most excellent of all the sciences. It is the central one around which every true science will revolve in its proper place; and happy is the man whose solar system of knowledge has Christ in the very center of it. Still, if it be so, I shall not cease to wonder and bless God that He has again brought wise men, like Saul of Tarsus, and like these wise men from the east, to worship this new-born Savior.

Notice also that these men were not only wise men, which is one cause of our wonder that they sought Christ, but *they lived far away in the east.* We do not know the distance they had traveled; but it does not matter; it was a long way, and probably a very difficult journey, in those days, at any rate. It did not seem likely, when this Child was born at Bethlehem, that worshipers should come outside of Judea, or that they should come from distant regions unknown to the Jews themselves; but yet God in His mercy called these men from the farthest east. Oh, that His love would light on some tonight who are strangers and foreigners, aliens from the commonwealth of Israel, perhaps without God and without hope in the world! May His grace call such! What a mass of people we are, and what odd people there must be here, whom none of us could describe! After this morning's sermon, somebody told me that, had I known the story of one of my hearers, I should not have dared to describe him as correctly as I did. Happily I did not know that hearer; I am glad that I did not; my message should come all the more distinctly as a voice from God to him, because it did so accurately describe him. But I will breathe this prayer, that somebody here, who is a stranger even to the very form of religion, someone who has never been in this house before, or in any other place of Christian worship, may be called by the mighty voice of God, attracted by the irresistible charms of Christ, and may come and believe in the Incarnate God who took our flesh at Bethlehem, that He might bear our sin, and bear us up to the throne of God with Himself. Here was the double wonder, then, about the magi coming to Christ, they were unlikely men from an unlikely place. As we think of them, we are constrained to say, as we have often sung—

> How sweet and awful is the place,
> With Christ within the doors,
> While everlasting love displays
> The choicest of her stores.

> Pity the nations, O our God!
> Constrain the earth to come;
> Send thy victorious Word abroad,
> And bring the strangers home.

And they were *singularly guided*, were they not? They were watching the midnight heaven, and they spied a strange star. According to astronomers, there was probably a conjunction of two planets about that date. When two planets were in conjunction in 1640, or about that date, it was said that such a conjunction must have taken place at about the time when Christ was born, and that the wise men may have thought it was a new star. I do not, however, think that that can have been the case. It was probably not simply a star, but a marked appearance which moved through the heavens. Well now, it was a strange thing that they should see this star, and more strange still that, seeing it, they should put this and that together, and by their astrology, for perhaps it was nothing better, infer that some wondrous personage was born away there in Judea, and they must needs go forth to find Him. They may have heard of the famous prophecy of Balaam; there might have been traditions in their country that the Coming Man was to be born in Judea. All that may have been, I do not know; but this I know, God miraculously sent this star. If men are not to be reached in any ordinary way, God's elect shall be brought to Him in an extraordinary way. If they are given to the study of the stars, God will write in that illuminated book which they are accustomed to read, and they shall there see a new letter, and learn something fresh concerning His will. I have known the Lord meet with men in the midst of evil, in the very act of sin. We have known men struck down by the most singular accidents and the most extraordinary concatenation of circumstances, men whom it seemed impossible to reach. Beloved, no man is beyond the reach of God. He has ways and means of enlightening the understanding, rousing the conscience, and renewing the heart, of which we know but little. "Remember that Omnipotence has servants everywhere," in the heaven above, and in the earth beneath, and in the waters under the earth. He has means of getting at the hearts of men, and He will do it. If it cannot be done anyhow else, He will make new stars; I was about to say, He will make new heavens and a new earth, but He will call His own. When Christ is born, the wise men from the east must come, and a star shall be sent to guide them. Perhaps, by some remarkable circumstances, you, my friend, are here tonight. It was very unlikely that you should be here; but you have come into the tabernacle that the grace of God may arrest you, that the hand of eternal love may be laid upon your shoulder, and that you may be taken prisoner for Christ, henceforth to be His servant, and His alone.

It is worth noticing, again, that these men *earnestly inquired.* Having once seen the star, they hurried off, no matter how long the journey, to find the new-born King, and they asked everybody to tell them the way to Him. They even went to the court of Herod to ask the way to find Christ. A man must have a deal of curiosity when he puts his head between the jaws of such a lion as Herod, in order to find what he wants to know. I wish that God would stir up that kind of curiosity and inquiry in many men's minds. The general way now is to put off the truth of God with a huff, to suppose that it is not worth looking into; but the claims of the eternal Son of God, the claims of His grace and of His throne ought not to be treated so. May God give back to the people a spirit of inquiry into the things of God, so that they may not be as indifferent as the masses of our fellow-citizens now are! May they begin to question, and say, "Which is the way to heaven? Who is this Christ? What is the plan of salvation?" If it be so, we shall soon have cause enough for joy, and we shall praise the sovereign grace of God.

Being inquirers, these men were *singularly unprejudiced.* They said, "Where is he that is born King of the Jews?" "Jews?" Who cared for Jews? Even in those days, Jews were the subject of contempt, for they had aforetime been carried captive into the east. Although they are the very aristocracy of God, His chosen people, yet the nations looked down upon the Jews. Judah was a little paltry territory, insignificant and small; and many asked with Sanballat, "What do these feeble Jews?" But here are men from a great empire, like Persia or Media, asking about the King of the Jews. Surely there are still some candid men about, some who will inquire after Christ, even though they have to ask of Methodists, and Baptists, and the like. Oh, that men could break through the foolish shell of prejudice to inquire if these things indeed are so! The time was when the very word "Evangelical" had a kind of contempt affixed to it; I am not sure that that time has yet quite passed. Yet, whatever others may say or do, let none of us be swayed by prejudice or disdain; but let us search and see whether these things are so.

And note again, that these men, being candid inquirers, were *wonderfully prompt*: "When Jesus was born, there came wise men from the east." Well now, I think that it would naturally strike you that, if a man was born a king, there would be time enough to pay him homage when he grew up. To bring gold, and frankincense, and myrrh, to a babe, does not always commend itself to wise men. Let us see the child become a chit, and the chit become a youth, and the youth become a man; then may we take this long journey to find out His Royal Highness. But, no; when the King was born, and the wise men came to Him, they must have started to find Him long before. I would that the Lord might put into the hearts of men today something like this energy and promptitude about divine things. If God really was incarnate, if He did come here in human form, oh, come, let us go and find Him! Let us bow at His shrine, and worship at His feet. Did He really die, and die for guilty men? Did He in their place and stead bear the desert of their sin? Come, let us seek this "Lamb of God, which takes away the sins of the world," and let us seek Him ere another sun has risen.

And then see, dear friends, how *supremely obedient* they were, how entirely surrendered to the divine impulse that moved them, for they hastened to do what they were bidden to do, and rejoiced as they bowed low before the new-born Child, worshiping and adoring Him. They were also *abundantly generous* with their offerings. They brought the best that they could find, gold, and frankincense, and myrrh, and they spread the royal gifts before the royal Child. Lord, send us converts like these wise men! Send us men and women, in great multitudes, who will cheerfully obey, who will find a delight in worshiping Christ, in paying Him homage, giving to His service, and in giving themselves to Him.

Thus I have tried to show you what the sovereign grace of God did when Christ was born. May the Lord in His mercy do the like to many here! Oh, how often has it happened that, when I least knew it, I was preaching to one who would become afterward one of our best helpers, one of our most earnest brothers, one of our most fervent sisters! I hope that I am speaking to some such tonight, utter strangers as yet, who will be brought into this church, or into some other church of Jesus Christ, and become not a whit behind the very chief of the apostles, though as yet they are not numbered with the household of faith.

The Nigh Ones Far Off

But now, in the second place, I have a sad task; the other was a glad task; but now I have the sad task in noticing THE NIGH ONES FAR OFF.

Here, first, we read that *many were troubled about Christ.* He was but newly born, and yet He troubled them. Herod was troubled, and all Jerusalem was troubled with Him. It is an unusual thing to hear of a king troubled by a babe. Proud Herod, the fire-eater, troubled by a babe in swaddling bands, lying in a manger? Ah me! how little is the real greatness of wickedness, and how small a power of goodness may bring it grief! Herod was troubled, and all Jerusalem with Him. So, when some people hear the gospel, and find that it has power in it, they are troubled. Herod was troubled, because he feared that he should lose his throne; he thought that the house of David, in the person of the new-born Child, would take possession of his throne; so he trembled, and was troubled. How many there are who think that, if religion be true, they will lose by it! Business will suffer. There are some businesses that ought to suffer; and as true godliness spreads, they will suffer. I need not indicate them; but those who are engaged in them usually feel that they had better cry out, "Great is Diana of the Ephesians," for they get their living by making and selling her shrines, and if their shrines are in danger and their craft is in danger, then they are troubled. There are such; I have known men, who have been leaders in sin, ringleaders in sin, and they have thought that they should lose some of their followers through Christ's coming; so they have been troubled.

But all Jerusalem was troubled with Herod. Why was that? It was most probably because they thought there would be contention. If there was a new King born, there would be a fight between Him and Herod, and there would be trouble for Jerusalem. So there are some men who say, "Do not bring that religion here; it makes such contention. One believes this, and one believes that, and another believes nothing at all. We shall have trouble in the family if we get religion into it." Yes, you will; that is acknowledged in the Scriptures, for our Lord came to bring fire on the earth. He has come, with a sword in His hand, on purpose to fight against everything that is evil; and there will be contention. Hence I do not wonder that the great lovers of ease are troubled.

But the fact is that many are troubled because the gospel interferes with their sin. "If I become a Christian, I cannot live as I have been accustomed to live," says one, "so I will not believe the gospel." The great argument against the Bible is an ungodly life. If you probe to the bottom of the matter, some sinful pleasure is the reason of many a man's infidelity. There is a practical reason against his repenting, he cannot give up his darling sin, he will not give that up; so he is troubled when Christ comes near to him. It is a terrible thing to cling to sin. That Spartan boy, who caught a young fox, and carried it in his bosom, and then, lest the schoolmaster should see it, and chastise him, allowed the fox to go on eating into his flesh till it ate into his heart, is like you. You are hugging this fox, this wolf, this asp, to your bosom all the while we are preaching to you. What comfort can we give you? Quit your sin, or quit all hope. Will you have your sin and go to hell, or will you leave your sin and go to heaven? You cannot have Christ and sin; the two are diametrically opposed. I will not mention what your sin may be; let your own conscience tell you that. You cannot continue in the practice of any known sin, willfully and deliberately, and yet find any comfort from the Word of God, or from the gospel. There must be, in your heart's intent and resolve, the quitting of sin, or there cannot be the finding of the Savior. I have told you before of the two Highlanders who wanted to row across a certain frith on one occasion. They had been largely helping themselves to whisky before they got into the boat, and they began to row, and they kept on rowing, but they made no progress. They could not understand how it was that, with all their rowing, they kept in the same position till one said, "Sandy, did you pull the anchor up?" No, he had never pulled the anchor up, so there they were, with the anchor down, and pulling away to no purpose. You must have that anchor up, young man, whether it is drink, or lust, or gambling, or pilfering. You are a fool if you pretend to row when you know that the anchor is still sticking in the mud.

Oftentimes, when a man is troubled about religion, he says, "If I become a Christian, I shall have to give up my pleasure"; not that true religion requires us to give up anything which is real pleasure; or, if it makes us give up what affords us pleasure now, it changes our tastes so that it would be no longer a pleasure could we indulge in what we once loved. True religion gives us new pleasures; it takes away our halfpence, and it gives us golden coin instead thereof. It does better than that, but I cannot employ a figure good enough to describe the change. True religion never was designed to make our pleasures less; and it does not make them less. But still some think that it will do so, and hence their trouble. You would be astonished if you knew why some men oppose true religion. The wife shall not go to a place of worship; there shall not be a Bible in the house; they will not have their boy attending a chapel where there is a prayer meeting or they will not allow the master where he is apprenticed to take the boy with him to the house of God. Men say and do all sorts of strange things when they are troubled by Christ; and it is not because they have any real ground for their perplexity. They are troubled about Christ very much for the same reason that Herod and Jerusalem were troubled about Him, certainly for no better reason.

Well now, this is very sad, that the gospel, which is meant to be good news to men should trouble them, that the heavenly offer of free grace should trouble them, that to have heaven's gate widely open before them should trouble them, that to be asked to wash themselves or to be washed in the blood of Christ should trouble them. Troubled by infinite mercy! Troubled by almighty love! Yet such is the depravity of human nature that to many who hear the gospel every day, it is still nothing but a trouble to them.

Now there is another case here. It is the same man in another character. *There is one who plays the hypocrite.* "Yes," he says, "there is one who is born King of the Jews. Will you wise men kindly tell me all about it? You say you saw a star. When did the star appear? Be very particular. Did you take note of its movements? You say *you* saw it, and *you* saw it, and *you* saw it. What time in the evening was it first visible? What day of the month did it appear?" Herod is very particular in getting all the information that he can about that star; and now he sends for the doctors of divinity, and the scribes, and the priests, and he says, "When ought this Messiah that you talk about to be born, and where ought he to be born? Tell me." Herod, you see, is a wonderful disciple, is he not? He is sitting at the feet of the doctors; he is willing to be instructed by the magi; and then he finishes up by saying to the wise men, "Go now; you go and worship the new-born King; you are quite right to have come all this distance to worship this Child. Be particular, too, to take notes as to where you find Him, and then come and tell me about Him, that I also may go and worship Him." So we always find that where Christ is, there is a Judas somewhere about. If the gospel comes to any place, there is a certain number of persons who say, "Oh, yes, yes, yes, we shall attend that place!" I know a certain town where there is one true preacher if the gospel, who has won many to Christ; but there are a great many who go there who know nothing at all about Christ. Of course they go to what is called "The Tabernacle" in that place, because it is the right place to attend. I know a town where there is one church, in which Evangelical doctrine is preached, and the good people all used to go to "St. Peter's." It was a kind of patent of respectability to have a pew at St. Peter's, because good Evangelical doctrine was preached there. Well now, that is just how it is with some persons nowadays. A certain number of people would think that all was wrong with them if they did not hear sound doctrine; but all the while they have made up their minds that sound doctrine shall never change their lives, and shall never affect their inward character. They are hypocrites, just as this man Herod was. They will not have Christ to reign over them. They do not mind hearing about Him; they do not mind acknowledging to a certain extent His rights; but they will not yield allegiance to Him, they will not practically submit to His rule, and become believers in Him. Am I not speaking to some such tonight? I know that I am. Dear friends, do not stop in that state, I pray you. You do not wish to be called a hypocrite; well then, if you cannot bear to be called by that name, do not be such a character. Be true; come to Christ, bow at His feet, accept Him as your Lord, trust Him to save you, and then rejoice in Him as your Savior and King.

But there were other characters beside the hypocrite who were troubled; and they were *the men who displayed their learning*. These were the scribes and the chief priests who looked in their Bibles, and turned up that passage of the prophet which said where Jesus was to be born. Now, I like these people for looking up their Bibles, and studying the Scriptures; but what I do not like in them is that, while they told Herod that Christ was to be born at Bethlehem, none of them said that they would go to Bethlehem and worship Him. Not a living soul of them, not a scribe or a chief priest said, "If this is the Messiah, who was to be born at Bethlehem—and this remarkable star makes us believe that it is even so—we will go with the wise men, and worship Him." No, not they; they were quite content to have the sacred roll, and read it, and know all about the truth, and yet to leave it there. I used to know, in my youth, certain very sound Calvinistic brethren. I fancy that they were a little too sound, certainly sixteen ounces to the pound with an ounce or two of bone thrown in; and, after they had had a glass or two of beer, they could talk over Scripture better than they could before. I think that the most of those people sleep in the dust. I hope that the whole tribe will; I mean those who live only upon talking sound doctrine without feeling the power of it. But nowadays I meet people "mighty in the Scriptures," yes, and very keen too upon doctrine, who—

Could a hair divide
Betwixt the west and northwest side,

as regards points of divinity; but as to charity to the poor, as to visiting the needy, as to caring for the souls of men, as to holy living, and as to prevalence in prayer with God, they are nowhere at all. I do pray you to dread a religion which is all in the book. You must have it in the heart; you must have it in the life or else this Child that was born at Bethlehem will only affect you so far that you turn over the Books of Scripture, and there is an end of the matter so far as you are concerned. Yes, yes, yes, know your Bible, that is good: but practice what your Bible tells you, for that is better. Yes, yes, yes, understand the doctrines of grace, be clear upon them; but love them, live them, for that is better far. Yes yes, yes, be a sound divine but let us see a holy humanity about you as well. God grant that it may be so! Otherwise, I tell you, your book learning will only leave you still an enemy of Christ.

The saddest point is that *none of these people sought Christ*; not Herod with his hypocrisy, nor Jerusalem with its troubles, nor the scribes and priests with their ancient knowledge; none of them sought Christ. May God grant that no hearer of mine may be in that black list! Oh, may we all seek Jesus! May we all find Him! May we find Him tonight! We shall seek and find Him if we really felt in our hearts that hymn that we sang just before the sermon—

I need thee, precious Jesus!
For I am full of sin;
My soul is dark and guilty,
My heart is dead within;
I need the cleansing fountain,
Where I can always flee,
The blood of Christ most precious,
The sinner's perfect plea.

There are two prayers with which I wish to close my discourse. One is, "Lord, bring the far-off ones near tonight!" May I beg the thousands of Israel present tonight to pray that prayer? You cannot tell for whom you are praying; you need not know. There may be persons here who are as far from God as they can be. To them I give this text, the word of our exalted Savior and Lord, "Look unto me, and be ye saved, all the ends of the earth; for I am God, and there is none else." Look, look, look, look! Sinner, look unto Him, and be saved!

There is life for a look at the crucified One,
There is life at this moment for thee.

"For thee." "For thee." Then look, look now, and find it to be even so.

"There is life at this moment *for thee.*"

The other prayer, and I ask my brothers and sisters here who have power in prayer to pray it, is, "Lord, bring the nigh ones really nigh; these many who are always in this house, and yet not in Christ!" No, I must not say these "many"; I mean, these few; for there are now few who are in that condition. Lord, bring them in! One came the other Monday, and said, "I am one of the few. I have been attending the Tabernacle for many years, and yet I have never told you that I have found the Savior"; and he came to confess his Master. There are some few of that sort still. Lord, bring them all in! You who are always hearers only, do you ever remember that text, "Many shall come from the east and west, and shall sit down with Abraham, and Isaac, and Jacob, in the kingdom of heaven. But the children of the kingdom"—that is, you people who have heard the gospel ever since you were children—"the children of the kingdom shall be cast out"—pushed aside—"cast out into outer darkness: there shall be weeping and gnashing of teeth"? Pray that it may not be so with one single hearer of mine tonight, for Jesus Christ's sake. Amen.

3

*Simeon's Swan Song**

Lord, now lettest thou thy servant depart in peace, according to thy word: for mine eyes have seen thy salvation (Luke 2:29–30).

If we are believers in Christ, we shall one day use words like these. Perhaps not just at present; and yet, possibly, sooner than some of us think, we shall gather up our feet in our bed, and we shall say with composure, "Lord, now lettest thou thy servant depart in peace, according to thy word."

See what death is to the believer. It is only a departure. It is a departure after a day of service. "Lord, now lettest thou *thy servant depart*. My day's work is done; let me now go home." With us who believe it will be a departure to a higher service, for we shall still be the Lord's servants even when we depart from this present sphere of labor. We shall go to do yet higher and more perfect work in the nearer presence of our Master. "His servants shall serve him; and they shall see his face." But death to the believer is only a departure from one form of service to another.

And, note, that it is a departing *"in peace."* We are at peace with God. We have—

> Peace! perfect peace! in this dark world of sin,
> The blood of Jesus whispers peace within!

As many as have believed in Jesus, have entered into rest. "Being justified by faith, we have peace with God"; we have joy and peace in believing; and, as we live in peace, we shall also die in piece. We shall remain in peace, and we shall depart in peace. A deep and holy calm will fill up our dying moments.

> It is enough: earth's struggles soon shall cease,
> And Jesus call to heaven's perfect peace!

---

* This sermon is taken from *The Metropolitan Tabernacle Pulpit*. It was intended for reading on Sunday, January 29, 1893, and was preached at the Metropolitan Tabernacle, Newington.

We shall be able to say, perhaps, when we come to die, what a dear friend of mine once said to me, when I went in to see him on his dying bed. A part of his affliction consisted in total blindness from what they call the breaking of the eye strings. Sitting up, although he could not see me, he moved his hand, and said—

> And when ye see my eye-strings break,
> How sweet my minutes roll!
> A mortal paleness on my cheek,
> But glory in my soul!

So will it be with us; we shall depart in peace. To the believer, death is not a thing to be dreaded; he even asks for it, "Lord, now *lettest* thou, permittest thou, thy servant to depart in peace. Grant it as a boon, vouchsafe it as a favor." Death to the sinner is a curse, but to the believer it is a form of benediction, it is the gate of life. To the sinner, it is a chain dragging him down to the unutterable darkness of the pit; but to the saint, it is a chariot of fire bearing him aloft to the heaven of light and love.

Note, also, that Simeon said, "Lord, now lettest thou thy servant depart in peace, *according to thy word*." Did you not notice, in our reading, what Luke says about Simeon in the twenty-sixth verse? "It was revealed unto him by the Holy Spirit, that he should not see death, before he had seen the Lord's Christ." The prophecy had been fulfilled, he had seen the Lord's Anointed; there was nothing more for him to desire upon earth, so he said, "Lord, now lettest thou thy servant depart in peace, according to thy word: for mine eyes have seen thy salvation." The reason for Simeon's holy calm, the cause of his finding death to be nothing but a departure out of this world, lies in this fact, that he could say, "Mine eyes have seen thy salvation." It is of that blessed fact that I am going to talk tonight as the Spirit shall help me.

I do not suppose that everybody here can say, "Lord, now lettest thou thy servant depart in peace." Some of you would not depart in peace if death came to you as you now are. Dear friend, if you are not prepared for death and judgment, you had better pray, "Lord, let me stop here till I have found peace with thee; and then let me depart in peace whensoever thou wilt."

I shall at this time take the innermost sense of the text, dwelling upon these words of Simeon, "Mine eyes have seen thy salvation." There were others who had seen the baby Christ with their natural eyes; but Simeon had seen, in the babe, Christ the salvation of God, not with his outward eyes, but with the inward perceptions of his spirit. I hope that many here present can say that they have seen, and do see, in Christ, God's salvation, and their salvation given to them of God. If so, I am sure that they feel ready to live, or ready to die; but if it be not so with any of you, if you cannot say, "Mine eyes have seen thy salvation," you cannot pray, "Lord, let thy servant depart in peace."

What, then, do these words mean, "Mine eyes have seen thy salvation"? I will try to explain their meaning in my discourse tonight; and when I have finished, I think you will see that there are these five things included in this utterance of old Simeon; first, here is *clear perception*; next, *perfect satisfaction*; then, *happy unbinding*; then, *dauntless courage*; and finally, *joyful appropriation*.

Clear Perception

The first thing for us to notice in Simeon's swan song is CLEAR PERCEPTION: "Mine eyes *have seen* thy salvation."

Some people are very hazy in their religion; they "see men as trees walking." They see things as we see them in London in a fog; that is to say, we do not see them clearly; we cannot see them distinctly; and yet we do see them after a fashion. The fault with a great many Christians, nowadays, is that they have only just light enough to see things as in a mist; they have not discerned clearly the sharply-cut image of the truth. But Simeon could say, not, "I think I see the salvation of God in Christ; I hope I do; perhaps I do; but he could say, "Mine eyes have seen thy salvation." Oh, happy are you, my friends, tonight, if you can distinctly and clearly see in Christ Jesus, the salvation of God!

True, Christ was but a baby then; and Simeon could easily hold Him in his arms; yet his faith could see everlasting salvation, *infinite salvation within God incarnate*. God has come into our world, and has taken upon Himself our nature. He that was born at Bethlehem was "very God of very God." He that trod the acres of Palestine, as He went about doing good, was the same who "was in the beginning with God," without whom was not anything made that was made. Christ is God. "The Word was with God, and the Word was God"; but it is equally true that "The Word was made flesh and dwelt among us (and we behold his glory, the glory as of the only begotten of the Father), full of grace and truth."

> It is my sweetest comfort, Lord,
> And will forever be,
> To muse upon the gracious truth
> Of thy humanity.
>
> Forever God, forever man,
> My Jesus shall endure;
> And fix'd on him, my hope remains
> Eternally secure.

Now, this Christ took upon Himself the sins of all His people. "Who his own self bore our sins in his own body on the tree." "The Lord hath laid on Him the iniquity of us all"; and sin being laid on Christ, it remained no more on those from whom He took it. He bore it that they might not bear it; He suffered the consequences of their sin that they might never suffer those consequences. Jesus made an atonement to the justice of God; He vindicated and honored the perfect law of the Most High. When I see Christ on the cross, Christ in the tomb, Christ risen from the dead. Christ at the right hand of God, I understand that He took away my sin. He died; He was buried; He came forth from the grave, having destroyed my sin, and put it away; and He has gone into the heavens as my Representative, to take possession of the right hand of God for me, that I in Him and with Him may sit there forever and ever. To me, Christ's sacrifice is a business transaction as clear and straight as mathematics could make it. I care not that men decry what they call "the mercantile theory of the atonement." I hold no "theory" of the atonement; I believe that the substitution of Christ for His people is the atonement for their sins; and that there is no other atonement, but that all else is theory. This is to me so clear, so true, so definite, that I can venture to say with Simeon, when I have seen Christ, especially Christ crucified, Christ glorified, "Mine eyes have seen thy salvation." Clear perception, then, is the first meaning of Simeon's words.

You young people, who have come to believe in Christ, get clear perceptions as to how Christ is God's salvation. Do not mix and muddle things up as so many do; but accept Christ as your Substitute, as "the Lamb of God, which taketh away the sin of the world." Believe that on the cross He paid your debt, discharged your liability, and bought you with a price, so that you are His, and His forever and ever. You will never have peace in death, I do not see how you are to have solid rest in life, without a sharp, crisp, clearly-cut idea of how Christ is the salvation of God. The bulk of people do not see it, and they therefore miss the comfort of it. The comfort of a man, immersed in debt, is assured if he has a friend who bears his burden, and pays his debt for him; then he feels that he is clear of all his former liabilities. I declare, before the living God, that I know of no solid comfort for my heart tonight but this, the chastisement of my peace was upon him, and with his stripes I am healed. May you get a clear perception of this great truth now!

Perfect Satisfaction

But, next, when Simeon could say, "Mine eyes have seen *thy salvation*," he had PERFECT SATISFACTION in Christ.

You observe, he takes Christ up in his arms, and says, "Mine eyes have seen," not, " a part of thy salvation," but "thy salvation." He is not looking to anything else for salvation, but only to that Man-child, seeing all that that Man-child will do, and bear, and suffer, recognizing in Him the two natures, the divine and the human; and as he clasps Him to his breast, he says, "Mine eyes have seen thy salvation. It is enough, I have here all that I want. Lord, now lettest thou thy servant depart in peace, according to thy word: for mine eyes have seen thy salvation."

Beloved friends, have you ever done with Christ what old Simeon did? "He took him up in his arms, and blessed God." All that you need to save you, lies in Him. I have known the Lord now for some forty years, or thereabouts. When I first came to Him, I came as a sinner, without any works of my own which I could trust, or any experience upon which I could rely; and I just rested my whole weight upon the finished work of Christ. Now, after forty years of service, and nearly forty years of preaching the gospel, have I any works of my own to add to what Christ has done? I abhor the thought of such a thing. Have I even the weight of a pin's head that I dare put into the scale with my Lord's merits? Accursed be the idea! More than ever do I sing—

> Nothing save Jesus would I know,

and nowhere would I rest but in Him alone. Now, dear Christian friends, I know you understand this, that Christ is an all-sufficient Savior, that He is all your salvation, and all your desire; and yet, perhaps, you are tempted at times to think that you must be this, or you must do that, or you must feel the other, or else Christ is of none effect to you. Think not so; but rest wholly and alone on Christ. Say, "I rest in Him, whether I am a saint or a sinner; whether I have bright frames or dark frames; whether I am useful, or whether I am defeated in my service. I have no more to trust in when I rejoice in the light of God's countenance than I have when I walk in darkness, and see no light. Christ is everything to me at all times; a winter Christ and a summer Christ; all my light when I have no other, and all my light when I have every other light."

> My hope is built on nothing less
> Than Jesus' blood and righteousness;
> I dare not trust the sweetest frame;
> But wholly lean on Jesus' name:
>> On Christ the solid rock I stand,
>> All other ground is sinking sand.

God bring you to this that you may just say, "I have seen Christ, mine eyes have seen God's salvation, I am perfectly satisfied; I want nothing else." Does a man pluck me by the sleeve, and say, "I will tell you something worth hearing"? My good fellow, go and tell it to somebody who wants to hear it; for I do not. I have heard all the news I want when I have heard of eternal salvation by Jesus Christ.

Happy Unbinding

Now, thirdly, notice that there is in Simeon's words, "Mine eyes have seen thy salvation," a kind of HAPPY UNBINDING. The man has been, as it were, bound; but he says, " Lord, now lettest thou thy servant *depart in peace.* Every fetter is broken now. I have seen thy salvation, Lord, I am not tied to life, nor tied to home, nor tied to comfort, nor tied even to Your temple. Now, Lord, I can go anywhere, departing in peace, for mine eyes have seen thy salvation."

Is not that a grand utterance of old Simeon? The most of us are in one way or another, and we find it hard to cut ourselves loose. With many of us, the first part of our life is often spent in tying ourselves down to this world; and by-and-by we feel that we are too much tied, bound, hampered, hindered; and we cry out, "How shall we get free?" The only way to get free is to get Christ. "If the Son shall make you free, ye shall be free indeed." If you take Christ in your arms, and say with Simeon, "Mine yes have seen thy salvation," you can then say, "Everyone else and everything else may go now."

> "Yea, shouldst thou take them all away,
>   Yet will I not repine;
> Before they were possessed by me,
>   They were entirely thine.

"And, as thou hast given me Christ, thou mayest do what thou wilt with me as to other things." Where Christ is not valued, gold becomes an idol. Where Christ is not prized, health becomes an idol. Where Christ is not loved, learning and fame become idols. Where Christ is not first and foremost, even personal beauty may become an idol. But when Christ becomes our all in all, because our eyes have seen His salvation, then the idols fall, Dagon is broken; we are emancipated; and we can say concerning all these things, "Ay, whether ye come or whether ye go, ye are not lords of the house; you are but comers and goers unto me henceforth and forever; for a clear conception that Christ is God's salvation, and a full grasp of Him as mine, have set my spirit free from every fetter that hitherto held me in captivity."

Dauntless Courage

I must not pause here, because I want you to notice how the being able to say, "Mine eyes have seen thy salvation," gives to a man DAUNTLESS COURAGE.

He who has once seen Christ as God's salvation is not afraid to see death. "Now," saith he, "I can look death in the face without dread, for I have seen God's salvation." He is not afraid of that tremendous judgment seat which will be set in the clouds of heaven, for He who will sit upon that judgment seat is God's salvation to us who believe. The man who is "looking unto Jesus" is not afraid of the day when the earth will rock and reel, and everything based upon it will shake to its destruction. He is not afraid of the star called Wormwood, nor of seeing heaven and earth on a blaze. "Mine eyes have seen thy salvation," saith he; and he bears this glorious vision about with him wherever he goes; it is more to him than any earthly talisman could be, it is more powerful than the most potent charm of the mystic or the magician. Such a man is safe; he must be safe; his eyes have seen God's salvation.

If you would have a courage of the truest kind that needs no stimulus of drink, and no excitement of the noise of trumpet and of drum, the calm courage that can suffer pain, that can bear rebuke, that can endure slander, that can stand alone, that could stand foot to foot with the infernal fiend himself, and yet not be afraid—if you would have such courage as that, you must get Christ in your arms; for then shall you say with Simeon, "Lord, come what may, I have nothing to fear, for mine eyes have seen thy salvation."

> Fearless of bell and ghastly death,
> I'd break through every foe;
> The wings of love, and arms of faith,
> Should bear me conqueror through.

Joyful Appropriation

I will not detain you much longer, for the time is well nigh spent; but I would say this one more thing, he who lays hold on Christ, makes a JOY-FUL APPROPRIATION of Him. His sight of Christ, his clear apprehension of what Christ is, is accompanied by a personal appropriation of Christ to himself. This is the matter that puzzles many. I have, during the past week, talked with several people who have heard from me concerning the way of salvation, and the preciousness of Christ, and the question of many of these inquirers has been this, "How can we get a hold of Christ? We believe that all you say about Him is true. Christ is God's salvation; but how can we take Him to be ours? You seem to treat Christ as if He were yours beyond all question. How can we learn to do the same?" My answer is, when you once know how the Savior saves, and how He is God's salvation, trust Him to save you. That trust grips Him, holds Him; and if you can hold Him, He is yours. We have certain rights of property extant among us, and a man may have to bring his title-deeds to prove that a house is really his own; but in the kingdom of grace, the only title-deed you want is that you have a hold of Christ. May I take Him, then, without any right? Yes, taking Christ gives you the right to take Him. "To as many as received him, to them gave he power to become the sons of God." There is a piece of bread on yonder table; I mean to have it for my own. It will be of no use for you to dispute with me about the matter, for I shall put it beyond all dispute. How? I shall take that bread in my hand. Well, you can wrench it from me. I shall do more than that; I shall eat it; I shall digest it; it will become a part of my own being. You will not get it away from me then; and I do not care if you go to law with me to try to get it. Possession is more than nine points of the law in such a case as that. Digestion and assimilation will be ten points of the law, certainly. Now, it is just so with Christ. Poor soul, take Him; believe Him; trust Him; appropriate Him. Trust Him more, and more, and more. The more the devil tries to take Him from thee, trust Him the more. Plunge yourself deeper and deeper still into this sea of salvation, and trust Christ still more.

Perhaps some one says, "But how may I know at first that I have a right to trust Christ? You have a right to trust Christ because you are commanded to do it. "Believe on the Lord Jesus Christ, and thou shalt be saved." "He that believeth and is baptized shall be saved." Make a dash for this great blessing. Take Christ tonight, whether or no; for, though it should seem like robbery to you to take Him, yet if you once have Him, he will never be taken away from you. Make a dash for Christ, I say, tonight, and take Him, saying, "I believe Him; I trust Him; I rest myself on Him." Heaven and earth shall pass away; but if you do trust Christ, you shall never be ashamed. There was never a man yet who dared trust Christ, and yet found that Christ was not equal to his need, or that He did not fully supply all his wants.

Simeon took Christ up in his arms. Somebody might have said, "Old man, what have you to do with the new-born King? Old man, you may be just and devout; but dare you handle the Incarnate God? Dare you fondle Him upon whose shoulders God has laid the key of His kingdom, whose name is called Wonderful, Counselor, the Mighty God, the Everlasting Father, the Prince of Peace? Dare you touch Him?" Yes, he dares do it; He takes Him up in his arms, he clasps Him to his heart, he rejoices over Him, he is ready to die with delight now that he has found Christ. Come, poor troubled ones, come tonight, and take Christ into your arms! And you, dear saints of God, who have done this long ago, do it over again! Take Him right up into your arms, as though He were still a babe. Take Him still to your heart, and say, "He is everything to me—my love, my hope, my brother, this blessed Incarnate God, who loved me, and gave Himself for me." If you can do this, it shall be well with you now, it shall be well with you in death, it shall be well with you throughout eternity.

Have I among my hearers any who are postponing this all-important business, putting it off till a more convenient season? Let me tell them something that ought to warn them of the risk they are running. Once upon a time, the prince of darkness said to the evil spirits under his command, "I want to see which of you can be my best servant. The gospel is being preached in various places, and many persons are hearing it, and I am afraid that my kingdom will suffer loss. Unless something can be done, I fear that many will desert from under the black flag, and enlist under the standard of Jesus of Nazareth. I would fain prevent this; which of you will help me?" Then up rose one, who said, "I will go forth, and say that the Bible is not true, that Christ is not God, and that what is preached is not the truth." But the great prince of the pit answered him, "You will not serve my turn just now. There are a few places where you will be very useful; but the most of those who are listening to this Word will scout you, and drive you back. You smell too much of the place where you go on my errands. You cannot do what I want now." Up stood another of the evil throng, and said, "Let me go, and I will bring forth certain new views of truth, and various fresh doctrines, and with these I will turn aside the thoughts of men from the old faith." But the prince of the power of the air replied, "You, too, are a good servant of mine, and you stand me in good stead at other times; but just now you are not the one for the task I propose." Then out spoke one, who said, "O prince of darkness, I think I am your good soldier on this occasion. Here am I, send me." "And what will you do?" said Beelzebub, "What will you do?" "I will go forth, and tell the people that the warnings of the preacher are true, and the voice of the gospel is the voice of God; I will not awaken and arouse them by any sort of opposition; but I will tell them that there is time enough, by-and-by, to attend to these things. I will bid them wait a little longer, and bide their time. I will put this word into the mouth of each one that he may say to the preacher, 'Go your way, for this time; when I have a convenient season, I will call for you.'" Then the grim master of the pit smiled, and said, "Go your way, my faithful servant, you are he that shall carry out my purpose right thoroughly, and so shall you foil the preacher, and the word that he utters shall fall to the ground." Is there not a message here for someone who is listening to my words?

"Mine eyes have seen thy salvation." How I wish that I could make some here, who do not know it, understand how divinely simple is the way of salvation! You are a sinner, guilty and condemned. Christ becomes a man, takes your sins, suffers in your stead. You accept Him to stand for you. You permit Him, by your faith, to be accepted as your Substitute, and His pains are put down instead of yours, and you are "accepted in the Beloved," and saved in Him. Oh, if you could but do this—and you may do it tonight before you leave this place, and I hope you will—if you do this, whether you be old or young, there will come to you a heart full of benediction for life, and the best of all preparations for death. Truly happy shall you be if you can say, "Mine eyes have seen thy salvation."

I seem as if I did not want to see anything else, after having seen Christ as God's salvation. There is a story told of Mahometans, who often are very fanatical, and do very strange and horrible things in fanaticism; but they have been known to go to Mecca, to see the tomb of their prophet, and when they have seen his tomb, they have taken a hot steel, and have drawn it across their eyes, that they might never see anything else, that indeed they might die with the view of the false prophet's tomb as their last sight. Now, that is not what we do; but still we would act in the spirit of it. "Mine eyes have seen thy salvation." People say, "See Naples, and die." They mean that it is so lovely that, when you have seen it, there is nothing more to see. See Christ, and what else is there to see? Now, whether you sail over the blue sea beneath a bluer sky, or dive into the deeps of this murky atmosphere, whether you are in a palace or in a dungeon, sick or full of bounding health, all these are items of small consequence. If your eyes have seen God's salvation, God has blessed you as only God can bless you. Go and live in peace, and go and die in peace; and praise the name of Him who gave you such a Savior to see, and the power to see Him. The Lord bless you, beloved! Amen and amen.

4

The First Five Disciples*

And the two disciples heard him speak, and they followed Jesus. Then Jesus turned, and saw them following, and saith unto them, What seek ye? They said unto him, Rabbi, (which is to say, being interpreted, Master,) where dwellest thou? He saith unto them, Come and see. They came and saw where he dwelt, and abode with him that day: for it was about the tenth hour. One of the two which heard John speak, and followed him, was Andrew, Simon Peter's brother. He first findeth his own brother, Simon, and saith unto him, We have found the Messias, which is, being interpreted, the Christ. And he brought him to Jesus. And when Jesus beheld him, he said, Thou art Simon the son of Jona: thou shalt be called Cephas, which is by interpretation, A stone. The day following Jesus would go forth into Galilee, and findeth Philip, and saith unto him, Follow me. Now Philip was of Bethsaida, the city of Andrew and Peter. Philip findeth Nathanael, and saith unto him, We have found him, of whom Moses in the law, and the prophets, did write, Jesus of Nazareth, the son of Joseph. And Nathanael said unto him, Can there any good thing come out of Nazareth? Philip saith unto him, Come and see. Jesus saw Nathanael coming to him, and saith of him, Behold an Israelite indeed, in whom is no guile. Nathanael saith unto him, Whence knowest thou me? Jesus answered and said unto him, Before that Philip called thee, when thou wast under the fig tree, I saw thee. Nathanael answered and saith unto him, Rabbi, thou art the Son of God; thou art the King of Israel. Jesus answered and said unto him, Because I said unto thee, I saw thee under the fig tree, believest thou? thou shalt see greater things than these. And he saith unto him, Verily, verily, I say unto you, Hereafter ye shall see heaven open, and the angels of God ascending and descending upon the Son of man (John 1:37–51).

---

* This sermon is taken from *The Metropolitan Tabernacle Pulpit* and was preached on Sunday morning, May 15, 1864.

If it be true that "order is heaven's first law," I think it must be equally true that variety is the second law of heaven. The line of beauty is not a straight line, but always the curve. The way of God's procedure is not uniform, but diversified. You see this with a glance, when you look at the *creation* around us. God has not made all creatures of one species, but He has created beasts, birds, fishes, insects, reptiles. All flesh truly is not the same flesh, neither are all bodies of the same order. The dull dead earth itself is full of variety. Gems sparkle not all with the same ray. The grosser and less precious rocks are marked and veined each one according to its own fashion. In the vegetable world what a variety of plants, shrubs, herbs, flowers, and trees, we have about us. In any one of the kingdoms of nature, whether it be the animal, vegetable, or mineral, you shall find so many subdivisions that it would need a long schooling to classify them, and a lifetime would not suffice to understand them all. Consider the winged creatures which flit through the air—what a diversity there is between the tiny humming bird, which seems to be but a living mass of gems, and the eagle which with soaring wing ascends to the sky and sports with the lightnings. The whole world is full of marvels, and no two marvels alike. You shall never be able to find God repeating Himself. This great Master may often paint two pictures which seem alike, but investigated with the microscope, what differences at once are revealed! Even those stars which seem to shine with rays of the same brilliance, are discovered by the aid of the telescope to be of different colors, forms, and orbits. Nay, even the very clouds are piled in varied forms, and the masses of nebula which make up the Milky Way are distinguishable from each other. God, in no instance that we can ever find, has used the same mold a second time. He is so affluent of designs, so abundant in the wisdom that devises, so prolific in plans, that even when He would accomplish the same end He chooses to take another road to it; and that new road is quite as direct as those by which He has formerly reached His purpose.

Certainly this observation holds good in *providence*. What strange diversity there has been in the dealings of God with His church! When He has chastened His people He has scarcely ever made use of the same rod twice. At one time Midianites shall come up and devour the land of Israel; another day the Philistines with their giants shall invade the country; then shall come the Babylonians and the Assyrians; anon the Roman power shall tread Judea under foot. And as the rods of his chastisement have been always different on the great scale, so you have found it on the little scale. God has seldom chastened you twice in the same way; you could trace diversities either in the manner of the blow or the instrument you were smitten with, or in the part of your mind which seemed to be the most affected by His chastisements. In deliverers, again, how great a variety— you scarce find two alike! God raises up a Gideon, but Jephthah is not like

Gideon, and Samson is not like Jephthah, nor is David to be compared to Samson or Gideon. They are all diverse; and their weapons are varied too. One man has to use an ass's jaw-bone, another must use a sling and a stone: one shall be content with the ox-goad, while another must draw the dagger. Different methods God ordains as well as different forms of man; and He delivers His people just according to His own will, but ever in a different form. Well may providence be so diverse when you consider that men themselves whom God uses to be His principal instruments are so unlike each other. There are not merely the great differences of race and of nationality, nor even the differences of birth and education, but we are all different in constitution—no two minds being alike. There is an individuality about every one of us which will prevent our ever being mistaken for anyone else. We might by accident be undistinguished, but let us be known, and very soon important differences will be discovered. God is ever the God of variety, and He will be so to the end of the chapter. He will do new things before he rolls up the book of history: we shall see new acts of the Lord; He will fight His battles after fresh methods, raise up deliverers different from any who have come before, and will exalt and glorify His name upon new instruments of music. Let us expect it. He is the God of variety, both in nature and in providence.

My text is a very clear illustration that the same law obtains in the *work of grace*. There is ever the same kind of operation, and yet ever a difference in the manner of operation. There is always the same worker in the conversion of the soul, and yet different methods for breaking the heart and binding it up again are continually employed. Every sinner must be quickened by the same life, made obedient to the same gospel, washed in the same blood, clothed in the same righteousness, filled with the same divine energy, and eventually taken up to the same heaven, and yet in the conversion of no two sinners will you find matters precisely the same; but from the first dawn of the divine life to the day when it is consummated in the noontide of perfect sanctification in heaven, you shall find that God works this way in that one, and that way in the other, and by another method in the third; for God still will be the God of variety. Let His order stand fast as it may, still will He ever be manifesting the variety, the many-sidedness of His own thoughts and mind. If then you look at this narrative—somewhat long, but I think very full of instruction—you may notice four different methods of conversion; and these occur in the conversion of the first five who formed the nucleus of the college of apostles—the first five who came to Christ, and were numbered among His disciples. It is very remarkable that there should be among five individuals four different ways of conversion. Were you, however, to examine any five persons, I suppose you would find similar disparity. Pick out five Christians indiscriminately and begin to question them how they were brought to know the Lord, you would find methods other than those you have here; and probably quite as many as four out of the five would be distinct from the rest.

The Conversion of the Two Disciples

The first case we have in the text is THE CONVERSION OF THE TWO DISCIPLES. One was probably John. We cannot speak with absolute certainty, but it was very probably John. We know it to have been the habit of this evangelist to omit his own name whenever he could. Sometimes he speaks of "that other disciple," when he means himself; and now and then he puts it, "that disciple whom Jesus loved." His love nurtured in him a kindly esteem of others, but an humble estimate of himself; while, therefore, he never omits to record the meed of praise others obtained from the lips of Christ, as often as he can he drops his own name. It is supposed then—and I think rightly—that one was John. The other was Andrew, Simon Peter's brother. The first two disciples are *the fruits of preaching*. May we not expect to find that the major part of our conversation in the result of the public ministry? "The two disciples heard John speak, and they followed Jesus." Let us offer a few words concerning this first matter. We expect, beloved, to see a great number of souls brought to God by the preaching of the truth. The preaching of the cross may be, and it actually is to those who perish, foolishness; but unto us who are saved, it is the power of God, and the wisdom of God. Wherever there is the most gospel preaching, you will find the most conversions. Many of our societies for carrying the gospel to the heathen forget their main work; and while setting up colleges, translating Bibles, and publishing tracts, they neglect to use this great hammer of God, this mighty battering ram which is to dash down strongholds. The preaching of the cross, the crying of, "Behold the Lamb of God!" This is God's appointed agency. Other labors are to be entered into, but this is His main and chief agency for the conversion of souls.

Observe in the case before us, *the preacher*. He was a man divinely illuminated. Jesus Christ came to John's baptism, but at first the Baptist did not know him. After awhile, however, when the descending Spirit marked out the Messiah, John then knew to a certainty that this was He of whom Moses in the law and the prophets did write. Ever afterward John's testimony was clear and bold. Though he ended his ministry with the loss of his head, he never lost the honesty of his purpose or the lucidness of his testimony; but he continued faithfully to declare that the Messiah had come. Brethren, it is of importance in the work of the ministry that the preacher be a God-illuminated man. Not that education is to be despised; on the contrary, we cannot expect the Spirit of God in these days to give to men the knowledge of languages if they can acquire that knowledge by a little perseverance. It is never the divine rule to work a superfluous miracle. With the faculties and powers we possess, we must yield up our members unto God as instruments of righteousness. So far then as the education of the man is concerned, we believe God leaves that with us, for if *we* can do it there is no need that any miracle should be wrought; but let the man be educated never so well, he is then but as the lump of clay; God must breathe into his nostrils the breath of spiritual life as a preacher, or else he will be of no service, but a dead weight upon the church of God. What shall we say then of those men who enter into a pulpit because the family-living is vacant, or because, forsooth, being too great fools for either the army or the law, they must needs be put where their livelihood can be more easily obtained—in the church? How crying is this sin in our times that men should have episcopal hands laid upon them, declaring that they are moved to the ministry by the Holy Spirit, when they know not whether there be any Holy Spirit, so far as any experimental knowledge of His power upon their own hearts is concerned! The day, I hope, is passing away, when men shall be more adroit at hunting the fox than at fishing for souls; and on the whole, God is raising up in this land a spirit of decision upon this point, that the Christian minister must be a man who knows experimentally in his own soul the truths which he professes to preach. God may convert souls, it is true, by a bad preacher. Why, if the devil preached, I should not wonder at souls being converted—if only the devil preached the truth. It is the truth, and not the preacher. Ravens, unclean birds though they be, brought Elijah his bread and his meat; and unclean ministers may sometimes bring God's servants their spiritual food; but for all that, unto the wicked God says, "What hast thou to do to declare my statutes?" The minister must be a God-taught man, whose eyes have been opened by the Holy Spirit. This, at least, is the standing rule—whatever exceptions may be pleaded.

Then, mark you, granted that this is the case, *we must not expect his ministry to be alike successful at all times*, for in the present instance, on one occasion John gave a very clear testimony for Christ, but none of his disciples left him to follow Jesus. The next time he preached he was successful, for two of his disciples joined the Master, though on the former occasion we read not that one of his hearers was led to declare himself on the Lord's side. My brethren, God suffers His ministers to cast the net sometimes on the wrong side of the ship. Even a whole night they may toil and take nothing; they may sow upon the barren ground, upon the highway, and among the thorns; they may cast their bread upon the waters, and as yet they may not find it, for the promise speaks of "many days." Still the minister must persevere. If souls are not saved today, they may be tomorrow. I was wondering, as I read this passage, whether there were some who heard last Sabbath in vain, who perhaps would hear to profit today. I was lifting up my heart in prayer to God that these words, "the next day after," might come true to some here. Whereas, the other day, I cried, "Behold the Lamb!" and you did not see Him or trust Him, I will repeat the cry, "Behold the Lamb!" again today. O that you may be led to follow Jesus!

When you have well considered the preacher and his success, I would have you observe *his subject*. How short the sermon—a rebuke to our prolixity. How plain it was—no difficult phrases—no high-flown elocutionary embellishments—no feats of oratory here; it is just, "Behold the Lamb!" But observe the subject—John preaches of Jesus Christ, of nothing else but Christ; and of Christ too, in that position and in that form in which he was most needed but least palatable. The Jews accepted Christ the Lion; they looked for the mighty Hero of the Tribe of Judah, who should break their bonds. Such Jesus was; but John did not preach Him as such; he preached Him as Christ the Lamb—the Lamb of God, the suffering, despised, meek, and patient sacrifice. He held Him up to the sons of men on this occasion as the great sin-bearer. He seems to have brought out most prominently in his own thoughts and before the minds of the people the picture of the paschal lamb and of the scape-goat; he dwelt upon this, that Jesus was the Lamb of God who takes away the sin of the world. If there are to be many conversions wrought in any place, the preacher must be a man taught of God, and he must persevere, even though he has been unsuccessful; but he must see to it that this be the staple of his sermons, the raw material out of which he makes every discourse—"Jesus, and Jesus the Lamb; Jesus the sin-bearer." He must ever be crying, "Ye sinners, see your sins laid on Him; you guilty, look to Him; trust Him; there is life in a look at Him. He has taken your sins and carried your sorrows; look to Him." Let the preacher stammer here, and he is undone. Let him be unsound on the atonement; let him speak in feeble strains, as though he apologized for so old-fashioned a doctrine, and you shall hear of no conversion from January to December; but let him hold this to be the first and most important truth, that Jesus Christ came into the world to be a sin-bearer for sinners, even the chief, and there must be conversions. God were not true to His promise, the truth were no longer the potent thing it has proved itself to be in the olden times, if souls were not quickened and turned to God by such a ministry as this. O you who preach the gospel, keep close to this, "Behold the Lamb of God!" You young men who stand up in the streets, make this your topic; and you who minister to the church of God, give them all the doctrines of the gospel, but still ever come back to this as the needle comes to its pole—"Behold the Lamb of God which takes away the sin of the world!"

In these two conversions by public ministry, it is interesting to observe the process. Carefully notice the narrative. *A spirit of inquiry was stirred up* in Andrew and his companion, and they began to follow Christ, not exactly as disciples as yet, but as searchers. If I may so say, they followed Christ's back; they had not come to see His face yet, or to sit at His feet, but they followed His back as some do who being impressed under the Word, have a desire after Christ, and intend to set about an honest investigation of His claims to their faith. While they are following behind Christ, *He turns around* and faces them. Oh! what a blessed turning for them. It was a blessed turning for Peter when the Lord turned and looked upon Him; and in this case while they are as it were following His back, He turns and *He looks upon them*. I cannot tell you how much love there was in His eyes. The love of a mother to her first child may perhaps picture the love of Jesus Christ to these His first disciples. He was God, He was man, He was God's own Son; but He had never been a Master of disciples until that moment. Now He springs to a rank which He had not obtained before. Now He has some who will call Him "Rabbi," and will be willing to be guided by His teaching. He looks round upon them. Even so, when inquiry is excited by the minister, and men begin to search, Jesus Christ looks upon them. With an eye of earnest affection He regards them and assists them in their search. Jesus put to them the question, *What seek ye?*—a very modest question, Notice it. It is the first word of Christ's minister. It is the first word I find Christ speaking at all in public—"What seek ye?" And was not it a very comprehensive question? "What is that you seek?" If there are any honest inquirers here after salvation, He puts the same question to you this morning—"What seek ye?" "Are you seeking pardon? You shall find it in Me. Are you seeking peace? I will give you rest. Are you seeking purity? I will take away your sin, a new heart will I give you, and a right spirit will I put within you. What are you seeking? Some solid resting place for your soul upon earth, and a glorious hope for yourself in heaven? Whatever you seek, it is here." What a text this might be for a missionary when first consulted by some of the awakened heathen, when he should say, "You are on the search after truth; now what is it that the human heart in its right state can possibly seek after—all that is to be found in Christ." Christ meets the man who is in an inquiring frame of mind by suggesting to Him further inquiry, He stirs up the heart; while the soul's fire is burning He puts fuel to the flame. They say, "Master, where dwellest thou?" And His answer to them is, *"Come and see."* This is just how the process of conversion is wrought in men's hearts; they want to know more of Christ, and He says to them, "Come and see!" You say you want purity—just try now the effect of the obedience of faith: see if it does not change your heart and renew your spirit. "Come and see." O you who are seeking and asking questions about Christ, and about His gospel, and His person, and His pedigree, "Come and see." The best way to be convinced of the potency of our holy gospel, is to try it for yourselves. If you are honest seekers, if the grace of God has made you so, then come and test, and try. "Blessed is every man that trusteth in him." This is our witness and our testimony; but if you want to be sure of it for yourselves, "Come and see." They took Christ at His word; they came and they saw. We are not told what they saw, but we are told what was the result: they stopped with Him that night, and they remained with Him all His days, and became His faithful disciples. O my dear friend, if you would but come and see Christ, if by humble earnest prayer you would give your heart to Him, and then trust in Him implicitly to be your guide, you would never lament the decision. If Jesus proves a liar to you, then desert Him; if His promises be not true, then stand no longer numbered with His disciples; but give Him a trial.

> O make but trial of his love!
> Experience will decide
> How blest are they, and only they,
> Who in his truth confide.

You see then the way in which God's grace works through the Word, excites a spirit of inquiry, then a still further inquiry, then the test of experience, and afterward leads to the giving up of the heart to Christ.

Private Instrumentality

The next case is a very different one. The third of Christ's disciples, one Simon Peter, was brought in by PRIVATE INSTRUMENTALITY, and not by the public preaching of the Word.

Observe the forty-first verse, "Andrew first findeth his own brother Simon, and saith unto him, "We have found the Messias, which is, being interpreted, the Christ." This case is but the pattern of all cases where spiritual life is vigorous. *As soon as ever a man is found by Christ, he begins to find others.* The word "first" implies that He did not give it up afterward—he *first* found his own brother Simon; how many he found afterward I cannot tell, but I will be bound to say that Andrew continued to be a fisher of men until he was taken up to the third heaven. He found very many after he had found Peter. The first instinct of the new-born life is to desire the good of others. I will not believe that you have tasted of the honey of the gospel if you can eat it all yourself. True grace puts an end to all spiritual monopoly. I know there are some who think there is no grace beyond the walls of their own tabernacle; beyond the range of the voice of *their* minister everything is unsound, unorthodox, pretentious perhaps, but still fatally delusive; they hold that all others are out of the bond of the covenant, and, not unlike those ancient wranglers in the land of Uz, they say, "*We* are the men, and wisdom will die with *us*." Surely God's people never talk in that fashion, or if they do, they are then speaking the language of Ashdod and not the speech of the child of Israel, for the Israelite's tongue drops with love, and his speech is full of the anxious desire that others may be brought in. Look at our apostle Paul. You shall never find stronger predestinarianism than you read in the ninth chapter of Romans, and yet what does he say? "His heart's desire and prayer to God for Israel is, that they may be saved. He had heaviness of heart, he says, for his brethren, his kinsmen according to the flesh. There was no man more anxious to convert souls than Paul, though there was no man more sound in the doctrine of the election of God. He knew it was not of him that wills, nor of him that runs, but yet he could say as Samuel did, "God forbid that I should sin against the Lord in ceasing to pray for you." See, then, that the first desire of a Christian is to endeavor to bring others to the Savior.

Relationship has a very stern demand upon our first individual efforts. Andrew, you did well to begin with Simon. I do not know, my brethren, whether there are not some Christians giving away tracts at other people's houses who would do well to give away a tract at their own—whether there are not some going out to the villages preaching who had better remain at home teaching their own children—or whether even in the Sabbath-school there may not be those who come before God to perform one duty, while their hands are stained blood-red with the murder of another duty. Your first business is at home. You may have a call to teach other people's children—that may be—but certainly you have an imperative call to teach your own. You may or you may not be called to look after the people of a neighboring town or village, but certainly you are called to see after your own servants, your own kinsfolk and acquaintance. Let your religion begin at home. We have heard of some people who export their best commodities—many traders do—I do not think the Christian should imitate them in that. At least, let the Christian have all his conversation everywhere of the best savor, but let him have a care to put forth the sweetest fruit of spiritual life and testimony at home, and in the circle of his own kinsfolk and acquaintance. Andrew, you did well first to find your brother Simon.

When he went to find him he may not have thought of what Simon would become. Why, *Simon was worth ten Andrews*, as far as we can gather from the evangelists. Peter was a very prince among the apostles; and with that ready tongue of his, and that bold, dashing, daring spirit, with that confident, resolute soul, there were none of them a match for Peter. John might excel in love, but still Peter was verily a leader among the apostles, and Andrew would but little compare with him. You may be yourself but very deficient in talent, and yet you may be the means of bringing a great man to Christ. Ah! dear friend, you little know the possibilities which are in you. You may but speak a word to a child, and in that child there may be slumbering now a great heart which shall stir the Christian church in years to come. Andrew has only two talents, but he finds Peter.

Andrew's testimony to Peter is worthy of remark. There was great modesty in it, and that, I dare say, commended it to Peter. He did not say, "*I* have found the Messias"—he says, *"We."* Whoever was the other disciple, he gives him his share of the discovery. Our speech never loses force by losing pride, but generally increases its power in proportion to its modesty, though that modesty must never interfere with boldness. His testimony was very plain and very positive. He did not beat the bush or hesitate, but it is just this—"We have found the Messias." Plain and unadorned was the statement, but very positive. He did not say, "I *think* we have," or "I *trust* we have," but *"we have,"* and this was just the thing for Simon Peter. Peter wanted positive and plain dealing, and he was a man who wanted it pushed home by a brother's friendly voice, or else it had little availed him to speak of Christ at all.

When he was brought to Jesus, observe the process of conversion. Jesus describes to him his present state. He said, "Thou art Simon, son of Jonas." Some interpret this, "Thou art Simon, the son of the timid dove." *He explains to him what he was*; shows that He knew him; that He understood both his boldness and his cowardice; both his rashness and his constancy; and then, when He had told him what he was, He gave him, a new name indicative of the nature which His grace would give—"Thou shalt be called Cephas, a stone." Now, this is the general plan of conversion; it is the plan in every case, really, though not apparently. Nature is discovered and grace is imparted. The old name we are taught to read with sorrow, and a new name is given to us, and we rejoice therein. There may be some here who have not been converted to God under the ministry but under the words of a Sunday school teacher, or a sister, or a friend. Thank God, and take courage; it does not matter how you are converted, so long as you are resting upon Jesus only; if you have not been a searcher of the Word, if Christ has never seemed to say to you, "Come and see"; yet if your nature has been changed, and you have received a new name—if there be a radical change in you, I will not inquire about the rest—you are a child of God. Though our case differs from the other, it is a rule with God that all shall not be precisely the same. That you are brought into the fellowship of the saints is an illustration of the unity of God's purpose; that there should be distinctive marks in your conversion is quite in harmony with the diversity of His operations.

By the Voice of Jesus

"The day following Jesus would go forth into Galilee, and findeth Philip, and saith unto him, Follow me." The fourth disciple is called without either the public Word or private instruction—he is called directly BY THE VOICE OF JESUS.

Now in truth all men are so called, for the voice of John or the voice of Andrew is really the voice of Jesus Christ speaking through their instrumentality; but in some cases no apparent instrumentality is used. We have known some who on a sudden have felt impressions, whence they came or whether they tended they did not know. In the midst of business we have known the workman suddenly check his plane—a great thought has entered into his brain; where it came from he could not tell. We have known a man wake up at midnight—he could not tell why, but a holy calm was upon him, and as the moon was shining through the window, there seemed to be a holy light shining into his soul, and he began to think. We have known such things to occur—surprising cases, when men have been planning deeds of vice. Was it not so with Colonel Gardner—that very night about to perpetuate a crime, and yet stopped by sovereign grace upon the very brink of it, without any apparent instrumentality? We cannot tell, brethren, when God may regenerate His elect, for though we are to use means, and cry to God to send forth laborers into the vineyard, yet the sovereign Lord of all will frequently work without them. The Word which has been heard in years gone by, the Scripture which was known in childhood, may by the direct power of the Holy Spirit, without any immediate apparent means, turn the man from darkness to light. Jesus Christ spoke but two words, but those words were enough—*"Follow me"*; and Philip at once obeyed. What preparation of heart there had been before, I cannot tell. What still small voice had been speaking before this in Philip's ear, we do not know. Certainly the only outward means was this voice of Christ, "Follow me." And there may be in this house some who will be converted this morning. You do not know why you are here, you cannot tell why you strayed in; but yet it may be—God knows—Christ would have you come here because he would come here Himself. Is not there something which invites a pause in that word "would," as we read it in this verse? "The next day following Jesus *would* go forth into Galilee." Is not there something of the divine necessity which we have often noticed in another place? "He must *needs* go through Samaria." Did not He feel instinctively that there was a soul there which He must meet with, and he must go after it, and speak the all-commanding, sin-subduing word? Perhaps this morning Jesus *would* come to the Tabernacle; Jesus *would* come here because he knows that Philip is come here too. Philip, where are you? You may have lived in sin and despised Christ, but if he says, "Follow me," I beseech you obey His word and follow Him. To follow Christ is the picture of *Christian discipleship in every form*. Follow Christ in your doctrines, believe what He teaches; follow Christ in your faith, trust Him implicitly with your soul; follow Him in your actions, let Him be your example and guide; follow Him in ordinances: in baptism follow Him, and at His table follow Him. To every deed of daring, to every place of spiritual communion, to the mountain in secret prayer, or to the crowd in open ministry, follow Him. According to your measure tread in the footsteps of your Lord and Master. And this, I say, may be directed to one who has had no other instrumentality used upon him, but just the mysterious voice of Christ—"Follow me." It was so with the third case. Perhaps of the three this experience is the highest. The first two were told, "Come and see," and they came to understand the value of Christ; but this one is made to follow—he carries out practically that which the others did but see. The second conversion before us attains a higher degree than the first; but this is the highest of all when the change of nature, as in the case of Peter, now leads to a change of action, as in the case of Philip, who arises and follows Christ.

A Composite Case or The State in Which He Then Was

I hope I have not wearied you, for there is yet the fourth case of the fifth disciple, which differs from them all—Nathanael. What shall we say of Nathanael? Was he converted by ministry? It does not appear. Was he converted by PRIVATE INSTRUMENTALITY? He was partly so. Philip finds Nathanael, but Philip's finding of Nathanael was not quite so effectual as Christ's finding of Philip. When Christ found Philip, Philip believed; but when Philip found Nathanael, Nathanael would not believe. He said, "Can there any good thing come out of Nazareth?" Philip is partly the instrument, but there is something more. Jesus Christ Himself shows His own power, BY TELLING TO NATHANAEL THE SECRETS OF HIS HEART; but still Nathanael's conversion to Christ seems to me to be PARTLY OWING TO THE STATE IN WHICH HE THEN WAS. He was already in some sense a saved man—he was a devout Israelite. He was a true seeker of the Messiah beneath the fig tree. Well, then, there were three things put together: here was a *preparation of heart* which was doubtless wrought of God; but this preparation did not bring him to Christ, though it made him ready for Christ; it brought him to God in prayer, but it did not bring him yet to the Lamb of God who takes away the sins of the world. Then came *Philip's instrumentality*, and then came *Christ's divine word, which convinced Nathanael and led him to put his trust in the Messiah.* This is a sort of composite case, and doubtless there are many in the church of God, who, if you should ask them, "How were you converted?" would be somewhat puzzled to give the answer. We find in our church meetings a very large proportion of people who say, "Well, I cannot trace my conversion to any one sermon—many sermons have impressed me—indeed most do. I cannot say, sir, that I was converted when I was a child, but I sometimes think I was, for even at that time I was the subject of many impressions, and I certainly did offer prayer." "Yet there was a time," they will tell you, "there was a time when I seemed to come out more distinctly into the light; and when I could say of Christ, 'Thou art the Son of God; thou art the King of Israel,' but I cannot say exactly when the sun rose." Now this, I think, was Nathanael's case. Perhaps trained and brought up by godly parents, he had been in the habit of prayer: that prayer was somewhat ignorant, but it was very sincere. He sought the solitude of his shady garden, and under the fig tree poured out his heart unto the Lord. That man is not saved. Ay! but there is a great part of the work done. Do not tell me that that man in his prayer has nothing in him more than the blasphemer. I tell you that he needs as much as the blasphemer does to have an effectual word from Christ, but still there is a preparatory work in this man which there is not even in Philip, or Simon Peter; there is a something, not meritorious, but still preparatory to the reception of the gospel of Christ; and when you labor for the conversion of such a man as this—and I do hope there may be some in this crowd—then it does not matter whether it be the ministry, or whether it be private instrumentality, there is sure to be good result, because there is good ground to begin with; God has already furrowed and plowed the soil, and so when the seed is scattered, there may be a little objection at first, but ultimately, it will take root. Be looking out then, dear friends, you who know how to talk to others about their souls, and wherever you see anything like devotion, even if it be mistaken and ignorant, look at that case; be specially hopeful about it, and try, if you can, to inform that person, "We have found him of whom Moses in the law and the prophets did write." Introduce Christ, talk of Jesus, bring these Nathanaels to Jesus—these who are like the honest and good ground, these men without guile or cunning—bring them to Jesus. Still, mark you, their prayers and your instrumentality will not be enough, unless Christ shall meet them with some startling, soul-discovering word, and shall say, "Before that Philip called thee, when thou wast under the fig tree, I saw thee." Ah! seeking soul, Christ sees you. Before you came here this morning Jesus saw you. Before you hear the challenge, "Look to Christ," Christ has looked upon you. If you are truly seeking in the loneliness of that upper room, or in that field behind the hedge, Jesus sees you. When you are by the wayside, and your heart is going up, "Lord, save me, or I perish," Jesus sees you. One of you has been writing to me this morning, and you say, "Pray for me that I may be saved, for I want to be saved." Ah! my friend, if you want to be saved, Jesus wants to save you, and so you are both agreed on that point. You, like to Nathanael, are seeking Him; and I come this morning, like to Philip, and I long to bring you to Jesus my Master. Oh! how I pray Him to speak to you, and if so, He will tell you that He knew you when you were dead in sin, and loved you, notwithstanding all; and therefore He brought you to this house to hear His Word.

Mark you, Nathanael's is the best case of the whole, he was favored above many. Who was the first man that ever had a promise from Christ? It was Nathanael. What was that? Why, that promise seems to me to be the sum of the gospel; or rather the token-promise of the gospel which every Christian should carry in his hand. Jesus said, "Because I said unto thee,

I saw thee under the fig tree, believest thou? *thou shalt see greater things than these.*" Nathanael was the first man who ever received a promise from the lips of the Lord Jesus when He was here on earth. O you seeking Nathanaels, I think this is a promise for you—"Thou shalt see greater things than these"—you shall see yourself pardoned; you shall see your prayers ascending Jacob's ladder, and blessings coming down from God to rest upon your soul.

I had hoped to have brought out many more points, but indeed the chapter is too full for one to handle it in so brief a time; you will observe, however, that I have given you just a glance at the surface of it, which will suffice to show that the means of conversion and the general tenor of conversion will be found to differ in each case. Perhaps Nathanael's is the highest of all; he receives Christ in a fuller way than any of the others, and he enjoys greater promises than they do, but still they are all genuine, though they are not one of them like the other, except that John and Andrew may be put together. Judge not therefore your conversion by its means or by its particular form, but judge it by its fruit. Does it bring you to Jesus? Are you depending upon Him now? If so, go your way; your sins, which are many, are forgiven; eat the fat and drink the sweet, for God accepts you; therefore do you rejoice. But, and if you have had a thousand conversions, if you are not resting on Jesus this morning, tremble, for your refuge is a refuge of lies, your hope is a spider's web—God deliver you from it, and bring you now to rest upon the finished work and the perfect sacrifice of the Lord Jesus, and then, with Andrew, and Peter, and John, and Philip, and Nathanael, you shall meet before the throne to praise Him who is the Son of God and the King of Israel. The Lord bless you, for Christ's sake. Amen.

5

Greater Things Yet.
Who Shall See Them?*

Jesus answered and said unto him, Because I said unto thee, I saw thee under the fig tree, believest thou? thou shalt see greater things than these. And he saith unto him, Verily, verily, I say unto you, Hereafter ye shall see heaven open, and the angels of God ascending and descending upon the Son of man (John 1:50–51).

We cannot help making a few remarks upon the narrative before we proceed to the distinct subject of discourse. Certain catch words are exceedingly worthy of notice, since they are abundantly full of instruction. When Nathanael had doubts as to whether the Messiah could come from Nazareth, Philip answered him, "Come and see." Now, those were the precise words which the Lord Jesus had Himself used to His earliest disciples when they began to follow Him: He also said to them, "Come and see." It is always safe for us to use over again words which God has blessed. Did the Master say, "Come and see"? Then we cannot do better than say what Jesus said, and use as near as possible the inspired expressions. Was that short sentence, "Come and see," made useful to other souls? Then those who would win souls cannot do better than use such gospel nets as have been tried and proved efficient in their own cases. Let none of us say that we cannot speak to others about their souls. There was one passage of Scripture which was the means of our conversion, and we cannot do better than repeat it in hearty tones to others, hoping that what God has blessed to us He may bless to others.

Short as was the inviting word, "Come and see," it was full of wisdom. Our Lord knows the philosophy of the human mind, and understands how best to produce faith in doubting hearts. "Come and see" is the sure cure

* This sermon is taken from *The Metropolitan Tabernacle Pulpit* and was preached on Sunday morning, June 8, 1879.

for unbelief. Some would tell doubters to sit down and think, and create faith by reflecting on the nature of things. We may long consider the state of man and the condition of our own nature before we shall thereby be enlightened as to the way of salvation. If we would judge of Christ we must consider Christ himself. He is His own best argument. The cobweb spinnings of conceited brains are easily broken through, but the facts, the indisputable facts of the Savior's life and death hold the understanding and the heart as with iron bonds. As our Savior said, and as His servant Philip said, even so say we to who would know Christ, "Come and see." Be not blinded by prejudices or misled by preconceptions, but read His story for yourselves. Seek His face for yourselves, and taste and see that the Lord is good. A personal relationship with Jesus is still the best evidence of His personal excellence and His power to save. Brother, do you have any doubt about the Master? "Come and see." Do you say within yourself, "Can He save such one as I am?" "Come and see." Do your sins cast you down and cause you to despair because you fear that even the Redeemer's blood cannot cleanse you? "Come and see." See Him as the Son of God and the Son of man, in His life of holiness and in His death of substitution; or see Him, if you will, up yonder at the right hand of God, making intercession for sinners; and as you are looking upon Him faith will steal in upon you through the power of the Holy Spirit. It is the mind's eye that must look, and by that look repentance and faith find entrance to the soul. "Come and see," for nothing will save a man but a personal sight of a personal Savior. Therefore, "Behold the Lamb of God which taketh away the sin of the world." The Lord Himself says, "Look unto me, and be ye saved, all the ends of the earth."

Our Lord Jesus Christ seems so to have approved the advice of Philip that He himself followed it up, and kept to the same form of expression. Did Philip say, "Come and see"? Then the Lord Jesus says, "Before that Philip called thee, when thou wast under the fig tree, *I saw thee*: thou hast come to see *me*, but I have already seen *thee*: there has been an antecedent look on my part: I saw thee before thou didst know anything about me, or hadst even heard of me from Philip." Nor does our Lord change His note even to the end of the conversation, but closes it by saying, "Because I said unto thee, I saw thee under the fig tree, believest thou? *thou shalt see* greater things than these." There, you see, is the great plan of salvation as it is wrought in us. First the Savior sees us, even when we are a great way off; then we come and see, and our hearts find rest in our Redeemer; and then in after days He gives us yet brighter and clearer views of Himself and of His kingdom. Oh, who would not come and see if this be so? If at our first coming and seeing we find life and rest, what must those still greater things be which are yet to be revealed? All that faith has yet discovered is but a foretaste and an earnest of more glorious sights which shall yet be opened up before our favored eyes, for Jesus himself said, "Thou shalt see greater things than these."

Other parts of the conversation are equally worthy of notice, as showing how fully the mind of the childlike Nathanael and the holy child Jesus responded to each other, as all true and childlike minds always do. Our Lord, as soon as He saw Nathanael, called Him "an Israelite indeed, in whom is no guile." He knew his simple, frank, open-hearted character, and He produced an example of it, for Nathanael did not blush and with mock modesty pretend to question the praise, but in the simplest and most unaffected manner he tacitly owned the description to be true, and said, "Whence knowest thou me?" He felt in his own conscience that he was a true son of that wrestling Jacob who became prevailing Israel, and in owning the title he made his words responsive to those of Jesus, for he said in effect, "True, I am an Israelite, but thou art the King of Israel." To this our Lord seemed to reply, "Thou art an Israelite, and thou hast owned Israel's King; and now thou shalt have Israel's privilege; for, like him, thou shalt see heaven opened and the angels of God ascending and descending upon the Son of man." Thus, as in water face answers to face, so did the heart of man to man in the relationship of these two guileless spirits. Their thoughts were so true that they harmonized like the parts of well composed music; their words so frankly bespoke their hearts that they answered to one another like the echo to the voice. This is the character of the relationship between our Master and His sanctified ones. He says, "I am the Good Shepherd," and the heart replies, "The Lord is my shepherd; I shall not want." The spouse says, "Yea, he is altogether lovely," and her bridegroom replies, "Thou art all fair, my love, there is no spot in thee." Our Lord calls us, "My love, my dove, my undefiled," and we being in full communion with Him reply, "My Beloved is mine, and I am his." As upon the sea in time of storm deep calls unto deep, so within the sanctified heart, in heavenly calm, truth calls unto truth: one word of love wakes up another, the commendation given by condescending love brings forth the praise of grateful affection. But to produce this mutual sympathy there must be a common character, a similar absence of guile, for this is the great condition of fellowship with Jesus. God's ways toward us are made to meet our own in a most instinctive way. "With the merciful thou wilt show thyself merciful; with an upright man thou wilt show thyself upright; with the pure thou wilt show thyself pure; and with the froward thou wilt show thyself froward." When His children open their hearts to Him He opens His mind to them; when they are true Israelites He gives them the true Israel's privileges; when they own Him to be a great and glorious King He makes them to see the great things of His kingdom. May it be ours through grace to be as little children, even as Nathanael was, for so shall we behold the kingdom of God.

With those prefatory remarks we come at length to consider the promise of our Lord Jesus to Nathanael. May the Holy Spirit instruct us thereby. I think I am warranted in saying that this is the Savior's first personal word of promise, and it is instructive that He gave it, not to the most talented, but to the most simple-hearted of His disciples. It was, moreover, no mean promise, but full of the largest conceivable meanings. "Thou shalt see greater things than these." Those must be very great things which were greater than what Nathanael had seen already; there is room for boundless expectation in the words. It was a promise which brought another linked with it as part and parcel of it. How often one divine blessing is like a link of a chain of gold and draws another with it: "Thou shalt see greater things than these" is followed by "henceforth ye shall see heaven open." The beauty of it in this instance is, that albeit Nathanael obtained a promise for himself at first, *"thou* shalt see," yet this drew on the promise for all his brethren, for the fifty-first verse does not run, "hereafter or henceforth thou shalt see heaven open," but hereafter "shall *ye* see heaven open." It is a great thing to receive a personal promise, but it is a greater thing still to secure a promise for all our Master's household. Happy Nathanael to have been the occasion for the proclamation of the opening of heaven and the commerce between heaven and earth, and the communion of saints with the things in heaven through their Mediator and Lord. This is the highest form of blessing when we are not only favored ourselves but are made the occasion for enriching others. Was not this the choice inheritance of Abraham, "I will bless thee, and thou shalt be a blessing"?

In considering the words which our Savior spoke to Nathanael, I should like you to notice first, *the favored man* to whom He spoke them; then *the gracious reward* which is described in them; and lastly, *the special sight* comprised in that reward, in all this may we be actual partakers, and not mere lookers on.

The Favored Man

Let us think of THIS FAVORED MAN. Nathanael was "an Israelite indeed, in whom is no guile." He was one of those who were not only of the chosen seed after the flesh, but after the Spirit. He was noted for being a simple-minded, unsophisticated person, as honest as the day. He was a truthful man, who knew nothing of policy, or craft, or double dealing, or reserve; a man out of whom all the twists had been taken, an upright and downright man, true to the core, and transparent as clear glass! Not a Jacobite, a child of the crafty supplanter, but an Israelite, an Israelite indeed, with the Jacob extracted out of him; pure, simple-hearted, ingenuous; not childish, but yet thoroughly childlike. To such a man the word was given, "Thou shalt see greater things than these."

Notice, first, that *he was a man who honestly made inquiries which fair-*

ly suggested themselves. Before he became a believer he did not, as some do, invent doubts and raise questions, which questions are merely raised for question's sake. He did not put queries to Philip which he could have answered himself, nor seek to entangle his instructor by artful speech. Nothing of the sort. He sought truth, not controversy and word-chopping. The two questions which he put came out of his heart, and were points which seemed to him to be vital. He did not go about to discover difficulties, but they occurred to him there and then, and he spoke them out with honest plainness. He was told that the Messiah had been found, and that He was Jesus of Nazareth. I doubt not he was well acquainted with Holy Writ, and he did not recollect any text in which the Christ was said to come out of Nazareth, and therefore he thought within himself, "I read of Bethlehem Ephratah that out of it shall he come forth who is to be ruler in Israel, but I do not remember a word concerning Nazareth." Without a moment's hesitation, he put the question, "Can any good thing come out of Nazareth?" It was a poor, miserable little place, of unsavory reputation. This, then, was a difficulty, a true and real difficulty, and he stated it, and was content to "come and see." When the Savior met him with the words, "Behold an Israelite indeed, in whom is no guile," he inquired, "Whence knowest thou me?" A most natural question to ask, for on its answer would depend the value of the words. Might it not happen that this accurate description of himself might have come to Jesus by report? If a correct description of Nathanael's character had reached the Savior by Philip or any other friend, then it did not prove anything; but if Jesus knew it by His own perception, and could read the character of a man to whom he was a stranger, then Nathanael knew what conclusion to draw. So he only asks the question because it ought to be asked, and does not lie upon the catch. How I love to meet with seekers who, though they are in difficulties, are willing to be led out of them, and are not studying how to invent more. Some of you cannot find peace in Christ because you willfully darken the atmosphere around yourselves; you are not assailed by doubt, but you invite doubt to assail you. You believe a great deal more than you like to own to; but do not want to believe, and are fishing for excuses for your unbelief. It is a sad state of mind for a man to be in, to be trying to discover reasons why he should not be saved, but that is what many are doing. That is a wretched mind which manufactures difficulties, and complicates plain things, because it cannot or will not take a thing in its straightforward, simple meaning, but must be puzzled and perplexed. Some men are too intellectual to believe the poor man's gospel, the run and read gospel, the gospel of "Believe and live"; they must needs be mystified, or excited, or driven to despair, or else they refuse to believe. There is a craving in some men for something that will appall them and fill them with despair. Is not this folly? Wait not for such sensations, I pray you. If you do, you will miss the blessing; but if, even while as yet you have not received full faith, you are honest enough to admit of none but honest difficulties, there is in you some good thing toward the Lord God of Israel, and the Lord be praised for it.

This Nathanael without guile was, next, *a man who honestly yielded to the force of truth.* Omniscience was proved to be an attribute of Christ to Nathanael by the pointed remark which Jesus addressed to him. What was Nathanael doing under the fig tree? "I know," says one, "for I have heard it said he was praying." Well, I did not say he was not praying, but I will defy anybody to prove that he was. What was Nathanael doing under the fig tree? We frequently read in the Talmudic writers of learned rabbis who studied the law under the fig tree. Was Nathanael studying the law? I did not say he was not, but I will defy anybody to prove that he was. What was he doing under the fig tree? There are only two people who could have told us, and both of these are silent on the matter. Both Jesus and Nathanael knew, but no one else. What he was doing under the fig tree we may not pretend to guess, for it is more instructive to leave it in the dark: our Lord's words were a kind of masonic sign to Nathanael, all the more conclusive because perfectly unknown and uninterpreted by the rest of mankind. Whether he was going to be baptized by John the Baptist, and sat down there to think of what he was doing; or whether, having been baptized, being on the way home, he suddenly felt an impression that he must sit in that place and wait, he knew not why—I may not profess to know, but it was an important movement to his own mind, and he remembered it as such. As soon as Jesus said, with a look, "When thou wast under the fig tree" Nathanael was startled into a conviction that his secret heart was known to Jesus. Under that tree he had done, or said, or thought a something known only to himself. How had the person before him known of that deed? It was true that this deed, or word, or thought under the fig tree was a pure, simple, and honest one, but how did Christ know? "If He knows that I was under the fig tree, and knows what I was doing there, and read my simple-minded, guileless character when I was there, then He is the Son of God, the King of Israel." This was Nathanael's immediate conclusion, and the argument was very clear and complete. Similar reasoning was used by others soon after Nathanael's conversion, and with the same result. When our Lord said to the woman of Samaria, "Go, call thy husband, and come hither," and she replied. I have no husband," he answered, "Thou hast well said, I have no husband: for thou hast had five husbands; and he whom thou now hast is not thy husband: in that saidst thou truly" Then the woman said, "Come, see a man, which told me all things that ever I did: is not this the Christ?" It was good argument, for omniscience proves Godhead. An omniscient one here in human flesh among the sons of men must be the Anointed of God; He must be the

Lord's Christ. I do not know whether Nathanael recollected the passage of Scripture, but this was the kind of argument used by the great God himself when He proved Himself to be God, in Isaiah 44:5. Notice how the passage, in many of its words, is parallel to our text. "One shall say, I am the Lord and another shall call himself by the name of Jacob; and another shall subscribe with his hand unto the Lord, and surname himself by the name of Israel. Thus saith the Lord the King of Israel, and his redeemer the Lord of hosts; I am the first, and I am the last; and beside me there is no God." And what is the proof of it? "Who, as I, shall call, and shall declare it, and set it in order for me, since I appointed the ancient people? and the things that arc coming, and shall come, let them show unto them." He challenges the false gods to tell what was being done in secret places, and what was to be done in the future, and He gives this as a proof of His Godhead. The heathen oracles attempted prophecy, because they saw how clearly it would prove the existence of their gods. Our Lord is a discerner of hearts, reading them as a scholar scans his book, and we know Him to be our God. Nathanael had drunk into the very essence of that wonderful 139th Psalm. No greater proof of Godhead can be given than the fact that all things are naked and open before the Lord. "O Lord, thou hast searched me. Thou knowest my downsitting and mine uprising, thou understandest my thought afar off." When I sat under the fig tree You read my heart. "Thou compassest my path and my lying down, and art acquainted with all my ways. For there is not a word in my tongue, but, lo, O Lord, thou knowest it altogether. Thou hast beset me behind and before, and laid thine hand upon me. Whither shall I go from thy spirit? or whither shall I flee from thy presence?" All this you see is a manifestation of Godhead. Nathanael therefore argued: "He saw me when nobody else did: He read my character in a simple act, an act which other people might have misunderstood, and thought me a fool for it: He perceived the uprightness of my heart, and now I know that He is certainly divine."

Notice, further, the blessing of our text comes to a man who *in simple honesty believes much upon the evidence of one assured fact*. It is proven that Christ can see in secret and read men's hearts: and from this, in addition to His divinity, Nathanael infers that "He is a great teacher," and he makes his first confession of faith by calling Him "Rabbi." He is sure that He who knows all things is worthy to be a teacher, and he gives Him the teacher's title. Then, as we have already said, he perceives that if He be omniscient He is divine, and he makes the confession, "Thou art the Son of God"; and, not satisfied with that, he sees that if He be indeed the Son of God, He must be Ruler and Lord, and therefore he calls Him the King of Israel. See here how he drinks into the spirit of the second psalm, where Son and King are the two great notes of harmony. "Yet have I set *my king* upon my holy hill of Zion. I will declare the decree: the Lord hath said unto me, Thou art *my Son*; this day have I begotten thee. Kiss *the Son* lest he be angry, and ye perish from the way, when his wrath is kindled but a little. Blessed are all they that put their trust in him." Gladly does Nathanael submit himself to the Son, and proclaim Him King of Israel. Was not this the first time that our Lord had been actually proclaimed as King since He had come into His public ministry? Was not this the answer to the wise men's question when they followed His star from regions far remote? Here was He who was born King of the Jews. This guileless man, who seemed to lack in shrewdness, had seen more than his fellows; his eye undimmed by falsehood or suspicion had seen the King, though His humiliation had unclothed Him of His royal mantle, and taken off His crown.

See, then, beloved, the gist of our first head is this. It is the pure in heart that shall see God. We must be honest and sincere; we must be clear of all subtlety and craft; we must be transparent as glass before Him, or else the Lord will not reveal Himself to us or by us. He loves the guileless and the true, and when He has made our eye single He will fill us with light, but not till then.

Note, again, that those who are ready to believe upon sure evidence—for Nathanael wanted that—are the men who shall see more and more. Nathanael did not require the evidence to be repeated to him again and again, he saw the argument at once, and yielded himself to it. When a point is once proved, it is proved, and there is an end of it. One conclusive argument is as good as twenty to an unsophisticated mind. Those who are willing to see shall see. Heaven is open to those from whose eyes the scales of prejudice are removed. The Lord manifests himself to those who manifest themselves to Him. If you will be Christians of the highest type you must be true to the core, and you must realize Christ and believe in Him with that mighty faith which sees Him, and realizes Him as close at hand. The presence and the power of Jesus must be undoubted by your soul, it must be as much a matter of fact to you as your own existence, and yours shall be the word which we are now about to consider—"Thou shalt see greater things than these."

The Gracious Reward

Let us now look at THE GRACIOUS REWARD. Only a few words upon it. Because this simple-hearted man had believed upon the one argument of the Lord's discernment of his heart he was favored with the promise of seeing greater things. By these words our Lord meant that *his perceptions would become more vivid.* Do you believe? You shall *see.* If we demand to see first we shall never believe; but if we are willing to believe we shall by-and-by see. There is a growth in faith which renders it not the less faith, and yet approximates it more and more nearly to sense. I mean "sense" in its best signification—so that what at first we believe, simply upon the testimony of God, we come by-and-by to believe upon personal experience. We believe until we so realize the object of faith that we look at the things which are not seen and see Him who is invisible. From this we go further still, until we both taste and handle of the good word of life, and faith becomes the substance of things hoped for. From looking to Christ we come to live, and move, and have our being in Him. The eye of faith gathers strength. At first it sees Christ through its tears, and that look saves the soul, though it perceives comparatively little of Him; but in after days the eye of faith becomes so powerful that it emulates that of the eagle, which can gaze upon the sun at midday. Thus faith becomes a second sight. Remember our Lord's words to Martha, "Said I not unto thee, that if thou wouldst believe thou shouldst see the glory of God?" "Believest thou? Thou shalt see."

This was not all our Lord's meaning. He virtually promised that Nathanael *should discover other truths than he as yet knew.* "Thou shalt see greater things than these." Now, what is there greater to be seen than the omniscience of Christ? "Such knowledge is too wonderful for me: it is high: I cannot attain unto it." Is there anything greater than this? Yes, so the Savior says. I suppose he means this: First, as you have seen mine omniscience in thine own case you shall go on to see it in the case of all mankind, for by my cross shall the thoughts of many hearts be revealed, and by my gospel shall men be revealed unto themselves. The Word of God is quick and powerful, and is a discerner of the thoughts and intents of the heart, and when Nathanael came to preach it in after years he found it so, and saw for himself that Christ read every man's heart. How wonderfully do we know this to be true in our time, and in this place, for here the Word finds us out and lays us bare to our own consciences. You have been startled in your seats sometimes; you have wondered how it could be, that not only in the gross has your experience been set before you, but even in the little details there have been minute touches which have amazed you with the distinctness of the divine knowledge. Our Lord did not say, "I saw thee under a tree," as if it might have been an oak or an olive, but he spoke definitely of "the fig tree." Even so does He cause his ministers to be very minute and particular, so that you wonder whence their knowledge comes. Now, when this is done on a large scale, as it is done whenever Christ is preached, then is it true that we see greater things than when for the first time we perceive that our own character is revealed.

He would see "greater things," next, because *he would see more of the Godhead.* Did you see omniscience? You shall see omnipotence. Did you discover that I could read your heart? Then shall learn that I can *change* your heart. Did you find that my eye could glance into the secret of your soul? You shall find my word casting out devils, and healing the sick, and hushing the tempests. You shall see clearer ensigns of my Godhead than this one experiment in the reading of the heart.

The Lord in calling Himself the Son of man, opens up to Nathanael one of those greater things. He had perceived Him to be the Son of God by his reading His heart, and it was a great thing to perceive the Godhead, but it was a greater wonder still to see that Godhead linked with humanity. Jesus, as Son of God, is glorious, but as at the same time Son of man He hath a double glory. Our Lord seemed to say to Nathanael, "Thou hast believed that I am the Son of God, thou shalt see the Son of man." And is this a greater thing? In one sense it is a descent for Jesus to be the Son of man, but yet you who know how to read the riddle aright will say that the Godhead is not half so wonderful in itself alone as when it comes to be united with our humanity. The incarnation has about it a mystery which is not seen even in the mystery of the Godhead. That there should be a God heathens might spell out, but that this God should come in human flesh among us—this is the mystery which angels desired to look into. Nor may I forget that the idea of our Lord as King *of Israel* is not so great as His connection with all nations, which is displayed in His title Son of man. He is not confined in His grace to Israel, as Nathanael probably thought, but He is brother to our entire humanity. Here was another of the greater things.

Note further, that Nathanael had only seen an opened heart but now he was to see *an opened heaven.* He had seen Christ's eye entering into his secrets, but he was now to see communications established between the lowly hearts of men and the secrets of heaven. He saw how Christ, as Son of God, dwelt among men; he is now to see how the abodes of God and man shall be blended in one, and high communion maintained between earth and heaven.

I come back to the one thought, that the sight of greater things is reserved for guileless believers. To those who already have much by faith more shall be given. Beloved, as a church and people, we have seen great things in this place in the work of the Lord among us; and we have lately celebrated with much joy and thankfulness the loving-kindness of the Lord to us: let us make this a new starting point, and hear the Lord say, "From this day will I bless you." We desire to see much greater things than we have known, and in order to this we must have more faith, and that faith must be more simple and childlike. The rule of the kingdom is that according to our faith so shall it be unto us. Unbelief bars the way of mercy. We tie the hands of Jesus if we have not faith. Is it not written, "He could not do many mighty works there because of their unbelief"? We must believe or we shall not be established, nor shall our work prosper. Whatever we have accomplished has been wrought by faith, but we believe that we might have done a hundred times as much if we had manifested a hundred times as much faith. May the Lord give us downright, honest, simple faith, and then we shall see greater things than these, for all obstacles will be removed, and eternal love will work wonders among us. Faith makes a man a fit instrument for God to use, and hence God does great things by him. If you are unbelieving God will no more use you than a warrior would use a reed for a weapon. He works no wonders by unbelieving ministers and unbelieving churches, for these are not prepared to be blest; they are not vessels fit for the Master's use; rust is upon them of the worst kind. When you heart is resting in the Lord, expecting to see His arm made bare, and quietly waiting to see how He will glorify Himself and fulfill His promise, then will you see greater things. When faith fails it disqualifies us and sets us aside even as in the case of Moses and Aaron, to whom the Lord said, "Because ye believed me not, to sanctify me in the eyes of the children of Israel, therefore ye shall not bring this congregation unto the land which I have given them."

We must have faith, for faith fulfills the condition which is virtually appended to every promise. Has not the Lord promised to answer the prayers of those who cry unto Him believingly? But as for the wavering He has said, "Let not that man expect to receive anything of the Lord." Is not faith our very life? "The just shall live by faith." Is it not our entrance into blessedness? For we see that Israel in the wilderness could not enter into Canaan because of unbelief. All the promises are for believers, and none for unbelievers. "As thou hast believed so be it unto thee," stands as the measure of blessing; there is no other limit.

Strong faith coupled with a guileless character brings a man into the special, complacent love of God; for, albeit that He loves all His elect, He does not delight in all alike. There were apostles among the disciples; there were three choice ones out of the twelve; there was one peculiar favorite out of the three. He is dearest to God who trusts Him most completely, and is most childlike and true. God will do most by that man who is most reliant upon Him, and most open with Him. David, who makes the Lord alone to be his confidence, is the man after God's own heart, and Abraham, who in faith could even give up his only son, is the friend of God. We shall never be full-grown with God until we become too little to dare to doubt, too insignificant to venture to question, too true to suspect the Lord. Increase in faith is the one thing needful to our advance in the divine life and work, and may the Holy Spirit work it in us for Christ's name's sake.

The Special Sight

We have only a minute or two in which to mention THE SPECIAL SIGHT which was promised to Nathanael. He was to see an opened heaven. The gates of glory are not only opened now to believers, but they are carried right away, and heaven is laid open to all its citizens, even to those who dwell below. This is a great joy to the believing heart, for free relationship with heaven is the delight of our spirit. I cannot enlarge upon this, which is worthy of another sermon, but I may not say less than this, that in Christ the saints are brought very near to God, for even now they have come to the heavenly Jerusalem. The franchise of the new Jerusalem is extended to these low-lying regions in which we sojourn. The veil is rent, and we have access to the holiest; the wall of separation is removed, and now the abode of the church below is an adjunct of heaven, a suburban district of the metropolitan city of the New Jerusalem. The gates shall not be shut, nor a division created, nor relationship suspended henceforth. Is not that a glorious thing, that in the person of Christ Jesus heaven is laid open to earth, and earth laid open to communications with heaven. Do you know that, beloved? It is a simple thing to talk of, but do you know it? Have you taken up your citizenship, so that you can say, "Truly our citizenship is in heaven"? While you are sitting under that fig tree do you know what it is to sit in the heavenly places, together with Christ? Are you risen and reigning with Him even now? If so, this is a joyful state of things, and one which should cause us much assurance. We are now dwelling in the house of our God, or at the very least we are sitting by the very gate of heaven. Our condition is known to the Lord, and He is near to help us; we suffer not unseen, and labor not unobserved. Nothing hinders God from succoring, nothing hinders us from securing His aid.

Then the Lord went on to promise that he should see that the relationship between heaven and earth by the way of the Mediator is not only possible, but actual. The ladder is set, and there are angels ascending and descending upon it. God does hear, and help, and speak with believing men of pure heart.

Observe that, according to the text, the angels ascend first. It does say, "Descending and ascending," as we might naturally suppose, but they ascend first, because when Jesus was on earth they were here already, and ascended at His bidding to carry His upward messages. When Jesus Christ was here He was never without His bodyguard of angels, and these were His messengers to the courts above. We, today, beloved, are surrounded by the forces of the Eternal: they have not to come to us for the first time; lo, they have those many years kept watch and ward around the fold of the redeemed; and when a new danger comes they are prompt to do the part of watchers and of guardians, and to carry tidings to the sentinels of heaven. Let us pray, for as we pray our prayers ascend to heaven, and our praises too. If we lead an angelical life our thoughts will always be going up to heaven, or returning thence. Beloved, have you realized this—that as you have believed in Christ upon the testimony of His word, you have now the right of access to the eternal throne at all times? You have but to speak and God will hear you. Some of God's people do not know much about this. Praying is a religious exercise with them, a very proper exercise, but it is not speaking with God; it is not doing business with God, and obtaining supplies at His hands. It is a ladder without angels, or, if you please, with ascending angels only, but none coming down with heavenly gifts. Beloved, I hope you have not fallen into this error. What, is not prayer real with you? Do you expect nothing from it? Would you send an angel on a fool's errand? Do these ascend to heaven in mere sport, and rush up and down to do nothing? Let us mean business when we pray, or we shall be mockers of the divine majesty. Too many come before God and ask for everything in general but nothing in particular, and they get but scant answers to their pointless prayers. Many more are very slack in prayer, and hence they starve their souls. Many angels must go up if many are to come down. Prayer must be constant and real with us. We should live as if we really had power with God, as if like Elias we could go the top of Carmel and pray a brazen heaven away and deluge the earth with showers of blessings. Are you unable so to live? Then the fault lies at your own door.

What was next? Nathanael was to see angels descending upon the Son of man, that is to say, he was to see heavenly spirits and blessings coming down to man by Jesus Christ. He who truly believes in Christ, and is without guile, shall have continual succors from on high: all heaven shall be opened to Him. God will help him by providence, will help him by grace, will help him by actual angels, and will help him spiritually by the all power which He has given unto Christ in heaven and in earth. How earnestly do I desire that this church this morning may see for itself what my eyes have seen for myself; for my faith sees heaven opened to supply the needs of Christ's work, and all the might of God working to achieve His purposes. I am just entering upon another work for God. We have had enough of these enterprises, say some, why not wait? I am forced to go forward and onward; I must go, nor do I fear, for lo, I see heaven opened, and the angels of God ascending and descending, by the way of Christ Jesus, to bring us succor. We may venture. There is no venture in it—we may trust God for anything, we may trust God for everything, and just go straight on. It looks like walking the waters sometimes to trust Christ, especially about gold and silver; but we need not fear, the waters shall be a sea of glass beneath our feet if we can but simply trust. But oh, we must purge ourselves, we must be without guile, there must be no self-seeking; there must be a simple-hearted desire for God's glory, and for nothing else; we must sink self, and Christ must reign, and then we must trust and go forward. I hope we are right in this matter, and if so, we shall see the salvation of God. Nothing can stop us. Behold, this day all things work together for good to them that love God. The stones of the field are in league with us, yea, it is not on earth alone that we find allies, but the stars in their courses fight against our foes, and all heaven is on the stir to befriend us in the service of God. See how the ladder swarms with coming and going angels! Heaven surrounds those who are doing heaven's work. God himself is with us for our Captain, and His host, which is very great, is round about us even as horses of fire and chariots of fire were round about the prophet. All things shall be given that are needed, and as our day our strength shall be. Brace yourselves up, my brethren, for a new endeavor. Be strong in the Lord and ye shall see greater things than these. Full of weakness, yet stand in *His* strength each one, and play the man. Say, "I can do all things through Christ that strengtheneth me." Omnipotence is waiting to gird your loins. Buckle it about you, and become mighty through God. Our Head, Christ Jesus, has all power in heaven and in earth, and that power He pours into all His members. By faith I commit myself, and I trust, also, my beloved church and friends, to further efforts for our Lord, relying upon His word, "Thou shalt see greater things than these," and fully believing that through Christ Jesus all the forces of heaven are in alliance with us, and the will of the Lord shall surely be accomplished.

6

*The Blind Beggar**

And they came to Jericho: and as he went out of Jericho with his disciples and a great number of people, blind Bartimeus, the son of Timeus, sat by the highway side begging. And when he heard that it was Jesus of Nazareth, he began to cry out, and say, Jesus, thou son of David, have mercy on me. And many charged him that he should hold his peace: but he cried the more a great deal, Thou son of David, have mercy on me. And Jesus stood still, and commanded him to be called. And they call the blind man, saying unto him, Be of good comfort, rise; he calleth thee. And he, casting away his garment, rose, and came to Jesus. And Jesus answered and said unto him, What wilt thou that I should do unto thee? The blind man said unto him, Lord, that I might receive my sight. And Jesus said unto him, Go thy way; thy faith hath made thee whole. And immediately he received his sight, and followed Jesus in the way (Mark 10:46–52).

This poor man was beset with two great evils—blindness and poverty. It is sad enough to be blind, but if a man that is blind is in possession of riches, there are ten thousand comforts which may help to cheer the darkness of his eye and alleviate the sadness of his heart. But to be both blind and poor, these were a combination of the sternest evils. One thinks it scarcely possible to resist the cry of a beggar whom we meet in the street if he is blind. We pity the blind man when he is surrounded with luxury, but when we see a blind man in want, and following the beggar's trade in the frequented streets, we can hardly forbear stopping to assist him. This case of Bartimeus, however, is but a picture of our own. We are all by nature blind and poor. It is true we account ourselves able enough to see; but this is but one phase of our blind-

---

* This sermon is taken from *The New Park Street Pulpit* and was preached on Sunday morning, August 7, 1859.

ness. Our blindness is of such a kind that it makes us think our vision perfect; whereas, when we are enlightened by the Holy Spirit, we discover our previous sight to have been blindness indeed. Spiritually, we are blind; we are unable to discern our lost estate; unable to behold the blackness of sin, or the terrors of the wrath to come. The unrenewed mind is so blind, that it perceives not the all-attractive beauty of Christ; the Sun of Righteousness may arise with healing beneath His wings, but 'twere all in vain for those who cannot see His shining. Christ may do many mighty works in their presence, but they do not recognize His glory; we are blind until He has opened our eyes. But besides being blind we are also by nature poor. Our father Adam spent our birthright, lost our estates. Paradise, the homestead of our race, has become dilapidated, and we are left in the depths of beggary without anything with which we may buy bread for our hungry souls, or raiment for our naked spirits; blindness and beggary are the lot of all men after a spiritual fashion, till Jesus visits them in love. Look around then, children of God; look around you this morning, and you shall see in this hall many a counterpart of poor blind Bartimeus sitting by the wayside begging. I hope there be many such come here, who though they be blind, and naked and poor, nevertheless are begging—longing to get something more than they have—not content with their position. With just enough spiritual life and sensitiveness to know their misery, they have come up to this place begging. Oh that while Jesus passes by this day they may have faith to cry aloud to Him for mercy! Oh may His gracious heart be moved by their thrilling cry, "Jesus thou Son of David have mercy on me!" Oh may He turn and give sight unto such, that they may follow Him and go on their way rejoicing!

This morning I shall address myself most particularly to the poor and blind souls here today. The poor blind man's faith described in this passage of Scripture is a fit picture of the faith which I pray God you may be enabled to exert to the saving of your souls. We shall notice *the origin of his faith, how his faith perceived its opportunity when Jesus passed by*; we shall *listen to his faith while it cries and begs*; we shall *look upon his faith while it leaps in joyous obedience to the divine call*; and then we shall *hear his faith describing his case*: "Lord, that I might receive my sight"; and I trust we shall be enabled to rejoice together with this poor believing man, when his sight is restored, as we see him in the beauty of thankfulness and gratitude follow Jesus in the way.

The Origin of This Poor Blind Man's Faith

First, then, we shall note THE ORIGIN OF THIS POOR BLIND MAN'S FAITH. He had faith, for it was his faith which obtained for him his sight. Now, where did he get it? We are not told in this passage how Bartimeus came to believe Jesus to be the Messiah; but I think we may very fairly risk a

you—it shall not be long ere the faith within you, which has been born by hearing, shall acquire strength enough to exercise itself to gain the blessing. That is the first thing—the origin of the faith of poor blind Bartimeus, it doubtless came by hearing.

His Faith's Quickness at Grasping the Gracious Opportunity

Now, in the next place, we shall notice his faith in ITS QUICKNESS AT GRASPING THE GRACIOUS OPPORTUNITY.

Jesus had been through Jericho, and as He went into the city there was a blind man standing by the way, and Jesus healed *him*. Bartimeus however seems to have resided at the other side of Jericho, therefore he did not get a blessing until Christ was about to leave it. He is sitting down upon his customary spot by the wayside where some friend has left him that he might remain there all day and beg, and he hears a great noise and trampling of feet, he wonders what it is, and he asks a passer-by what is that noise? "Why all this tumult?" And the answer is, "Jesus of Nazareth passeth by." That is but small encouragement, yet his faith had now arrived at such a strength that this was quite enough for him, that Jesus of Nazareth passes by. Unbelief would have said, "He passes by, there is no healing for you; He passes by, there is no hope of mercy; He is about to leave, and he takes no notice of you." Why, if you and I needed encouragement, we should want Christ to stand still; we should need that someone should say, "Jesus of Nazareth is standing still and looking for you"; ay, but this poor man's faith was of such a character that it could feed on any dry crust on which our puny little faith would have starved. He was like that poor woman, who when she was refused, said, "Truth, Lord, I am but a dog, yet the dogs eat the crumbs which fall from the master's table." He only heard "Jesus of Nazareth passeth by"; but that was enough for him. It was a slender opportunity. He might have reasoned thus with himself, "Jesus is passing by, He is just going out of Jericho; surely He cannot stay now He is on a journey." No, rather did he argue thus with himself, "If He is going out of Jericho, so much more the reason that I should stop Him, for this may be my last chance." And, therefore, what unbelief would argue as a reason for stopping his mouth did but open it the wider. Unbelief might have said, "He is surrounded by a great multitude of people, He cannot get at you. His disciples are round about Him too, He will be so busy in addressing them that He will never regard your feeble cry." "Ay," said he, "so much the greater reason then that I should cry with all my might"; and he makes the very multitude of people become a fresh argument why he should shout aloud, "Jesus of Nazareth have mercy upon me." So, however slender the opportunity, yet it encouraged him.

And now my dear hearers, we turn to you again. Faith has been in your heart perhaps for many a day, but how foolish have you been; you have not availed yourself of encouraging opportunities as you might have done. How many times has Christ not only passed by, but stopped and knocked at your door, and stood in your house. He has wooed and invited you, and yet you would not come, still trembling and wavering, you dare not exercise the faith you have, and risk the results and come boldly to Him. He has stood in your streets—"Lo these many years," until the poor blind man's hair would have turned gray with age. He is standing in the street today—today He addresses you and says, "Sinner come to Me and live." Today is mercy freely presented to you; today is the declaration made—Whosoever will, let him come and take of the water of life freely." You poor unbelieving heart will you not, dare you not take advantage of the encouragement to come to Him? Your encouragements are infinitely greater than those of this poor blind man, let them not be lost upon you. Come now, this very moment, cry aloud to Him now, ask Him to have mercy upon you, for now He not only passes by, but He presents Himself with outstretched arms, and cries, "Come unto me, and I will give you rest, and life, and salvation."

Such was the encouragement of this man's faith, and I would that something in the service of this morning, might give encouragement to some poor Bartimeus, who is sitting or standing here.

Listen to the Cry of Faith

In the third place, having noticed how the faiths of the blind man discovered and seized upon this opportunity, the passing by of the gracious Savior, we have TO LISTEN TO THE CRY OF FAITH. The poor blind man sitting there, is informed that *it is* Jesus of Nazareth. Without a moment's pause or ado, he is up and begins to cry—"Thou Son of David, have mercy upon me—thou Son of David, have mercy on me." But He is in the middle of a fair discourse, and His hearers like not that He should be interrupted—"Hold your tongue, blind man. Begone! He cannot attend to you." Yet what does the narrative say about him? He cried the more a great deal"; not only cried he more, but he cries a *great deal more*. "Thou Son of David, have mercy on me." "Oh," says Peter, "do not interrupt the Master, what are you so noisy for?" "Thou Son of David, have mercy on me," he repeats it again. "Remove him," says one, "he interrupts the whole service, take him away," and so they tried to move him; yet he cries the more vigorously and vehemently, "Thou Son of David, have mercy on me—thou Son of David, have mercy on me." I think we hear his shout. It is not to be imitated; no *artiste* could throw into an utterance such vehemence or such emotion as this man would cast into it—"Thou Son of David, have mercy on me." Every word would tell, every syllable would suggest an argument, there would be the very strength, and might, and blood, and sinew of that man's life cast into it; he would be like Jacob wrestling with the angel, and every word would be a hand to grasp him that he might not go. "Thou Son of David, have mercy on me." We have here a picture of the power of faith. In every case, sinner, if you would be saved, your faith must exercise itself in crying. The gate of heaven is to be opened only in one way, by the very earnest use of the knocker of prayer. You cannot have your eyes opened until your mouth is opened. Open your mouth in prayer, and He shall open your eyes to see; so shall you find joy and gladness. Mark you, when a man has faith in the soul and earnestness combined with it, he will pray indeed. Call not those things prayers that you hear in the churches. Imagine not that those orations are prayers that you hear in our prayer meetings. Prayer is something nobler than all these. That is prayer, when the poor soul in some weighty trouble, fainting and athirst, lifts up its streaming eyes, and wrings its hands, and beats its bosom, and then cries, "Thou Son of David, have mercy on me." Your cold orations will never reach the throne of God. It is the burning lava of the soul that has a furnace within—a very volcano of grief and sorrow—it is that burning lava of prayer that finds its way to God. No prayer ever reaches God's heart which does not come from our hearts. Nine out of ten of the prayers which you listen to in our public services have so little zeal in them, that if they obtain a blessing it would be a miracle of miracles indeed.

My dear hearers, are you now seeking Christ in earnest prayer? Be not afraid of being too earnest or too persevering. Go to Christ this day, agonize and wrestle with Him; beg Him to have mercy on you, and if He hear you not, go to Him again, and again, and again. Seven times a day call upon Him, and resolve in your heart that you will never cease from prayer till the Holy Spirit has revealed to your soul the pardon of your sin. When once the Lord brings a man to this resolve, "I will be saved. If I perish, I will still go to the throne of grace and perish only there," that man cannot perish. He is a saved man, and shall see God's face with joy. The worst of us is, we pray with a little spasmodic earnestness and then we cease. We begin again, and then once more the fervor ceases and we leave off our prayers. If we would get heaven, we must carry it not by one desperate assault, but by a continuous blockade. We must take it with the red hot shot of fervent prayer. But this must be fired day and night, until at last the city of heaven yields to us. The kingdom of heaven suffers violence, and the violent must take it by force. Behold the courage of this man. He is hindered by many, but he will not cease to pray. So if the flesh, the devil, and your own hearts should bid you cease your supplication, never do so, but so much the more a great deal cry aloud, "Thou Son of David have mercy on me."

I must observe here the simplicity of this man's prayer. He did not want a liturgy or a prayer book on this occasion. There was something he needed, and he asked for that. When we have our needs at hand they will usually suggest the proper language. I remember a remark of quaint old Bunyan, speaking of those who make prayers for others, "The apostle Paul said he knew not what to pray for, and yet," says he "there are many infinitely inferior to the apostle Paul, who can write prayers; who not only know what to pray for, and how to pray, but who know how other people should pray, and not only that, but who know how they ought to pray from the first day of January to the last of December." We cannot dispense with the fresh influence of the Holy Spirit suggesting words in which our needs may be couched; and as to the idea that any form of prayer will ever suit an awakened and enlightened believer, or will ever be fit and proper for the lip of a penitent sinner—I cannot imagine it. This man cried from his heart, the words that came first—the simplest which could possibly express his desire—"Thou Son of David, have mercy on me." Go and do likewise you poor blind sinner, and the Lord will hear you, as He did Bartimeus.

High over the buzz and noise of the multitude and the sound of the trampling of feet is heard a sweet voice, which tells of mercy, and of love, and of grace. But louder than that voice is heard a piercing cry—a cry repeated many and many a time—which gathers strength in repetition; and though the throat that utters it be hoarse, yet does the cry wax louder and louder, and stronger still—"Jesus, thou Son of David, have mercy on me." The Master stops. The sound of misery in earnest to be relieved can never be neglected by Him. He looks around: there sits Bartimeus. The Savior can see him, though he cannot see the Savior: "Bring him hither to me," says He; "let him come to me, that I may have mercy on him." and now, they who had bidden him hold his clamor change their note, and gathering around him they say, "Be of good cheer; rise, he calleth thee." Ah, poor comforters! they would not soothe him when he needed it. What cared he now for all they had to say? The Master had spoken; that was enough, without their officious assistance. Nevertheless they cry, "Arise, he calleth thee"; and they lead him, or are about to lead him, to Christ, but he needs no leading; pushing them aside he hurls back the garment in which he wrapped himself by night—no doubt, a ragged one—and casting that away, the blind man seems as if he really saw at once. The sound guides him, and with a leap, leaving his cloak behind him, waving his hands for very gladness, there he stands in the presence of Him who shall give Him sight.

How Eagerly He Obeyed the Call

We pause here to observe HOW EAGERLY HE OBEYED THE CALL. The Master had but to speak, but to stand still, and command him to be called, and he comes. No pressure is needed. Peter need not pull him by one arm, and John by the other. No; he leaps forward, and is glad to come. "He calls me, and shall I stand back?"

And now, my dear hearers, how many of you have been called under the sound of the ministry, and yet you have not come? Why is it? Did you think that Christ did not mean it when He said—"Come unto me all ye that labor and are heavy laden, and I will give you rest?" Why is it that you still keep on at your labors and are still heavy laden? Why do you not come? Oh, come! Leap to Him that calls you! I pray you cast away the raiment of your worldliness, the garment of your sin. Cast away the robe of your self-righteousness, and come, come away. Why is it that I bid you? Surely if you will not come at the Savior's bidding, you will not come at mine. If your own stern necessities do not make you attend to His gracious call, surely nothing I can say can ever move you. O my poor blind brothers and sisters! You who cannot see Christ to be your Savior, you that are full of guilt and fear, He calls you,

> Come ye weary, heavy laden,
> Lost and ruined by the fall.

Come you that have not hope, no righteousness; you outcast, you despondent, you distressed, you lost, you ruined, come! come! today. Whoever will, in your ears today does mercy cry, "Arise, he calleth *thee!*" O, Savior! call them effectually. Call now: let the Spirit speak. O Spirit of the living God, bid the poor prisoner come, and let him leap to lose his chains. I know that which kept me a long time from the Savior was the idea that He had never called me; and yet when I came to Him, I discovered that long ere that He had invited me, but I had closed my ear; I thought surely He had invited everyone else to Him, but I must be left out, the poorest and the vilest of them all. O sinner! if such be your consciousness, then you are one to whom the invitation is especially addressed. Trust Him now, just as you are, with all your sins about you, come to Him and ask Him to forgive you; plead His blood and merits, and you cannot, shall not plead in vain.

Listen to His Suit

We proceed toward the conclusion. The man has come to Christ, let us LISTEN TO HIS SUIT. Jesus, with loving condescension takes him by the hand and in order to test him, and that all the crowd might see that he really knew what he wanted, Jesus said to him—"What wilt thou that I should do unto thee?" How plain the man's confession, not one word too many, he could not have said it in a word less—"Lord that I might receive my sight." There was no stammering here, no stuttering, and saying, "Lord I hardly know what to say." He just told it at once—"Lord that I might receive my sight."

Now if there be a hearer in this house who has a secret faith in Christ, and who has heard the invitation this morning, let me beseech you go home to your chamber, and there, kneeling by your bedside, by faith picture the Savior saying to you—"What wilt thou that I should do unto thee?" "Fall on your knees, and without hesitation tell Him all, tell Him you are guilty, and you desire that He would pardon you. Confess your sins; keep none of them back. Say, "Lord, I implore you pardon my drunkenness, my profanity, or whatever it may be that I have been guilty of"; and then still imagine you hear Him saying—"What wilt thou that I should do unto thee?" Tell Him, "Lord I would be kept from all these sins in the future. I shall not be content with being pardoned, I want to be renewed"; tell Him you have a hard heart, ask Him to soften it; tell Him you have a blind eye, and you cannot see your interest in Christ. Ask Him to open it; confess before Him you are full of iniquity and prone to wander; ask Him to take your heart and wash it, and then to set it upon things above, and suffer it no longer to be fond of the things of earth. Tell it out plainly, make a frank and full confession in His presence; and what if it should happen, my dear hearer, that this very day, while you are in your chamber, Christ should give you the touch of grace, put your sins away, save your soul, and give you the joy to know that you are now a child of God, and now an heir of heaven. Imitate the blind man in the explicitness and straight-forward of his confession and his request—"Lord, that I might receive my sight."

Once again, how cheering the fact, the blind man had no sooner stated his desire than immediately he received his sight. Oh! how he must have leaped in that moment! What joys must have rushed in upon his spirit! He saw not the men as trees walking, but he received his sight at once; not a glimmer, but a bright full burst of sunlight fell upon his benighted eyeballs. Some persons do not believe in instantaneous conversions, nevertheless they are facts. Many a man has come into this hall with all his sins about him, and ere he has left it has felt his sins forgiven. He has come here a hardened reprobate, but he has gone away from that day forth to lead a new life, and walk in the fear of God. The fact is, there are many conversions that are gradual; but regeneration after all, at least in the part of it called "quickening," must be instantaneous, and justification is given to a man as swiftly as the flash of lightning. We are full of sin one hour, but it is forgiven in an instant; and sins, past, present, and come, are cast to the four winds of heaven in less time than the clock takes to beat the death of a second. The blind man saw immediately.

And now what would you imagine this man would do as soon as his eyes were opened. Has he a father, will he not go to see him? Has he a sister, or a brother, will he not long to get to his household? Above all has he a partner of his poor blind existence, will he not seek her out to go and tell her that now he can behold the face of one who has so long loved and wept over him? Will he not now want to go and see the temple, and the glories of it? Does he not now desire to look upon the hills and all their beauties, and behold the sea and its storms and all its wonders? No, there is but one thing that poor blind man now longs for—it is that he may always see the man who has opened his eyes. "He followed Jesus in the way." What a beautiful picture this is of a true convert. The moment his sins are forgiven, the one thing he wants to do is to serve Christ. His tongue begins to itch to tell somebody else of the mercy he has found. He longs to go off to the next shop and tell some work fellow that his sins are all pardoned. He cannot be content. He thinks he could preach now. Put him in the pulpit, and though there were ten thousand before him, he would not blush to say, "He hath taken me out of the miry clay, and out of the horrible pit, and set my feet upon a rock, and put a new song into my mouth and established my goings." All he now asks is, "Lord, I would follow You whithersoever You go. Let me never lose Your company. Make my communion with You everlasting. Cause my love to increase. May my service be continual, and in this life may I walk with Jesus, and in the world to come all I ask is that I may live with Him."

You see the crowd going along now. Who is that man in the midst with face so joyous? Who is that man who has lost his upper garment? See he wears the dress of a beggar. Who is he? You would not think there is any beggary about him; for his step is firm and his eyes glisten and sparkle, and hearken to Him; as he goes along, sometimes he is uttering a little hymn or song; at other times when others are singing, hearken to his notes, the loudest of them all. Who is this man, always so happy and so full of thankfulness? It is the poor blind Bartimeus, who once sat by the wayside begging. And do you see yonder man, his brother, and his prototype? Who is it that sings so heartily in the house of God, and who when he is sitting in that house, or walking by the way is continually humming to himself some strain of praise? Oh! it is that drunkard who has had his sins forgiven, it is that swearer who has had his profanity cleansed out, it is she who was once a harlot, but is now one of the daughters of Jerusalem—'tis she who once led others to hell, who now washes her Redeemer's feet and wipes them with the hairs of her head. Oh, may God grant that this story of Bartimeus may be written over again in your experience, and may you all at last meet where the eternal light of God shall have chased away all blindness, and where the inhabitants shall never say, "I am sick."

7

The Centurion: or, An Exhortation to the Virtuous*

And when they came to Jesus, they besought him instantly, saying, That he was worthy for whom he should do this: for he loveth our nation, and he hath built us a synagogue. Then Jesus went with them. And when he was now not far from the house, the centurion sent friends to him, saying unto him, Lord, trouble not thyself: for I am not worthy that thou shouldest enter under my roof: wherefore neither thought I myself worthy to come unto thee: but say in a word, and my servant shall be healed. For I also am a man set under authority, having under me soldiers, and I say unto one, Go, and he goeth; and to another, Come, and he cometh; and to my servant, Do this, and he doeth it. When Jesus heard these things, he marveled at him, and turned him about, and said unto the people that followed him, I say unto you, I have not found so great faith, no, not in Israel (Luke 7:4–9).

This centurion certainly had a high reputation. Two features of character blend in him which do not often meet in such graceful harmony. He won the high opinion of others and yet he held a low estimation of himself. There are some who think little of themselves; and they are quite correct in their feelings, as all the world would endorse the estimate of their littleness. Others there are who think great things of themselves; but the more they are known, the less they are praised; and the higher they shall carry their heads, the more shall the world laugh them to scorn. Nor is it unusual for men to think great things of themselves because the world commends or flatters them; so they robe themselves with pride and cloak themselves with vanity, because they have by some means, either rightly or wrongly, won the good opinion of others. There are very few who

---

* This sermon is taken from *The Metropolitan Tabernacle Pulpit* and was preached at the Metropolitan Tabernacle, Newington, in 1864.

have the happy combination of the text. The elders say of the centurion, that he is worthy; but he says of himself, "Lord, I am not worthy!" They commend him for building God a house; but he thinks that he is not worthy that Christ should come under the roof of his house. They plead his merit; but he pleads his demerit. Thus he appeals to the power of Christ, apart from anything that he felt in himself or thought of himself. O that you and I might have this blessed combination in ourselves; to win the high opinion of others, so far as it can be gained by integrity, by uprightness, and by decision of character, and yet at the same time to walk humbly with our God!

Now there are three things I shall speak about tonight, and may God make them profitable. First, *here is a high character*; secondly, *here is deep humility*; and, thirdly, here is, notwithstanding that deep humility, *a very mighty faith*.

High Character

To begin, then, dear friends, here is A HIGH CHARACTER; let us thoroughly appreciate it, and give it a full measure of commendation.

When preaching Jesus Christ to the chief of sinners, we have sometimes half dreamed that some who are moral and upright might think themselves excluded: they ought not so to think, nor is it fair for them to draw such an inference. We have heard the whisper of some who have said they could altmost wish that they had been more abandoned and dissolute in the days of their unregeneracy, that they might have a deeper repentance, and be witnesses of a more palpable and thorough change, so that they might never have cause to doubt of the triumph of grace in their experience. We have heard some even say, "I could have wished that I had groveled in the very mire of sin; not that I love it, on the contrary, I loathe it, but because had I then to be rescued from such a course of life, the change would be so manifest and apparent that I should never dare to ask myself whether I was a changed man or not. I should feel it, and see it in my everyday course and conversation." Dear friends, if anything we have ever said should have led you into this mistake we are sorry for it: it was never our intention. While we would open the gates of mercy so wide that the greatest blasphemer, the most unchaste and the most debauched, may not be without hope; yet we never want to shut those gates in the face of such as have been brought up in a godly manner, and through the providence of God and the checks of education, have been kept from the grosser vices. On the contrary, we thought that when we opened it for the worst there would be room for the best; and if Noah's ark took in the unclean, certainly the clean would not be afraid to enter. If Jesus Christ was able to cure those who were far gone in sickness, you might infer that He would certainly be able to heal those who, though they were sick, might not be so far advanced in disease. Besides, a little reflection may suggest to you that the penitence of contrite believers is not regulated by the extent of their crimes against what you call the moral code. It is one thing to estimate sin by its apparent turpitude, and another and an infinitely better thing to have the eyes of the understanding enlightened, to see sin in its infinite malignity as it appears in the light of heavenly purity and perfection, which proceeds from the throne of God, or as it is reflected from Mount Calvary where the amazing sacrifice of Christ was offered. What! do you think the whitewashed sepulcher of a Pharisee's heart less loathsome to the Almighty than the open pollution of a Magdalen's life? Or, in the matter of experience, could the recollection of a thousand debaucheries give such a melting sense of contrition as a sight of the Crucified one? O friends, let me remind you of the words of Jesus, "When he"—the Spirit of truth—"is come, he will reprove the world of sin, and of righteousness, and of judgment: of sin, because they believe on me." That one sin of unbelief is such a concentration of all wickedness that it could outweigh the crimes of Sodom and Gomorrah, and make them more excusable in the day of judgment than the men of Capernaum who saw the mighty works of Christ and repented not. That one sin of unbelief is so heinous that the groans of the whole creation were but pitiful sighs to deplore it; and rivers of tears were but a weak tribute to lament it. However, as mistakes do arise, and misapprehensions will take place, let us have a few words concerning a high character *in the sight of men.*

Such a character among your fellow creatures may be gained in any situation. The centurion was a soldier—a profession of life not altogether the most propitious for moral excellence; though there have been in the army some of the brightest saints that ever lived. He was a soldier moreover in a foreign country—not the place where he was likely to win esteem. He was there as one of the representatives of a power which had conquered Judea, and had treated it with great cruelty; yet, notwithstanding the prejudices of race and nationality, this man's kindness of disposition and goodness of conduct had won for him the esteem of others. Moreover, being a commander of soldiers, naturally every act of violence would be set down to him. Whatever might be done by his hundred men would be laid to the captain, so that his was a condition of peculiar difficulty, and yet, not withstanding this, the elders said, "He is worthy." Let none of you despair! Wherever you may be placed, a noble character may be earned. You may serve God in the most menial capacity; you may compel your very foes to own your excellence; you may stand so unblamably before men, and you may walk so uprightly before God, that those who watch for your halting may bite their lips with disappointment, while they shall not have a single word to say against you except it be touching the religion of your God and King. Let no man, wherever he may be thrown—though he be surrounded by those who tempt him—despair, especially if the grace of God be in him. Let him pray like Joab that he may have favor in the eyes of his Master, and expect to win it.

This centurion must have been a man of sterling worth. He was not merely quiet and inoffensive like some men who are as insipid as they are harmless. Though a high character may be won, it cannot be won without being earned. Men do not get character among their fellows by indolence and listlessness, or by pretensions and talk. Action! action!—this is what the world wants; and there is more truth than we have dreamed of in Nelson's aphorism, "England expects every man to do his duty." Certainly, men will not speak well of you unless you do well. This centurion did so, for you will observe that they said he was worthy—which must have signified that he was just in his dealings and generous in his habits, or they would not have thought him worthy.

It would appear, too, that his *private temperament* as well as his *public spirit*, contributed to the estimation in which he was held. You will notice in the circumstances which bring him before us, how his tender feelings, and his intense anxiety, were drawn out on behalf, not of a child, but of a servant, peradventure of a slave! And then we might have thought it had been enough to have said that the man was highly valued by his master; but the expression is one of fondness; he was *"dear unto him."* The fidelity of the servant may be implied, but it is the amiability of the master which is most prominent, chiefly arrests our attention. Nor need we overlook the fact that Matthew lays an emphasis upon the servant being "at home" under his master's roof. We know that the Romans were not remarkable for the kindness they showed to their dependents; often they were merely looked upon as slaves. Why, in our own days, and in the midst of our boasted civilization, when Christianity has exerted a salutary influence upon all our social relations, I suppose it is not uncommon for domestic servant to go home to her parents' house in the case of sickness. It is not every good man among us, I fear, whose gentleness would equal that of the centurion in the love which he bears to his servant, and the comfort he provided for him in his own house.

Next to this, you will observe his *generosity*. It is not, my dear friends, by occasional deeds of showy luster, but by the habitual practice of comely virtues that a worthy character is built up. A thousand kindnesses may be nestling beneath the soil, like the many-fibered root of a gigantic tree, when it is said, *"He loveth our nation"*; and then the conspicuous fruit appears in its season: "He hath built us a synagogue." This example of liberality is spoken of as a mere supplement. The Jewish elders do not say, "He loveth our nation"—*for*—but "he loveth our nation, *and* he hath built us a synagogue." This last was a visible token of innumerable good offices which had already won their secret esteem before it bloomed in an open reputation. I have heard all sorts of men praised, and I have noted the qualities which win the plaudits of the crowd. Even the high and haughty have some to praise them; but I think I never heard a stingy man praised, or one who was perpetually guilty of meanness. Let him have whatever virtues he may, if he lack liberality, few, if any, will speak well of him. Let me commend to the Christian, liberality in all his actions, and benevolence in all his thoughts. This may sound commonplace; but I am persuaded that the little tricks in trade, those little savings of the pence, those sharp dealings, are just the things which bring religion into disrepute. It were infinitely better that the Christian should pay too much than too little. He had better be blamed for a excess of generosity, than take credit to himself for a rigid parsimony. Rather let him become now and then the dupe of an impostor, than shut up the bowels of his compassion against his fellowman. I would seek, Christian man, to win a noble character. I cannot see how you can do so, except you should put generosity into the scale, and enroll it in the list of your virtues.

A high character, when earned, is very useful. I am saying this because some might imagine that, in the preaching of the gospel, we put the base and the wicked before those who have walked uprightly. A good character, when earned, a good reputation in the esteem of men, may win for us, as it did for this centurion, kind thoughts, kind words, kind acts, kind prayers. There is many a man who will pray for you if he sees you walk uprightly; ay, and your very adversary, who would otherwise have cursed you, will find the curse trembling on his tongue. Though he would fain rail, yet does he hate his breath, abashed at your excellencies. Let the Christian labor so to live that he shall not lack a friend. "Make to yourselves friends of the mammon of unrighteousness," is one of Christ's own precepts. If to stoop, to cringe, to lie, wins you friends, scorn to do it; but if with uprightness before God, you can still mingle such affection and generosity toward men, that you shall win their suffrages, do it I pray you. The time may come when their sympathy shall befriend you.

But, remember, and here I close this point, however good your character, or however excellent your repute, not one word of this is ever to be mentioned before the throne of the Most High. Job could say when he was talking with his adversaries "I am not wicked"; he could boast in his excellencies, as he did; but in the presence of God how he changed his note: "Now mine eye seeth thee: wherefore I abhor myself and repent in dust and ashes." Coming before the Lord, we must all come as sinners. When on your knees, you have nothing to boast of more than the veriest *roué*, or the man who has sinned against his country's laws. There, at the foot of the cross, one needs the cleansing blood as much as the other. At mercy's gate we must alike knock, and we must be fed by the same generous hand. There are no degrees here: we enter by the same door; we come to the same Savior; and we shall ultimately—glory be to His name—sit together in the same heaven whether we have earned a good repute or no; whether we have crept into heaven, as the thief did, at the eleventh hour, or through forty-and-five years of public service earned the applause of men, as did Caleb the son of Jephunneh.

> Nothing in my hand I bring,
> Simply to thy cross I cling,

must be the common footing, and the like confession of both before the God of mercy. Thus much by way of tribute to the high character of the centurion and the high motives to emulate it.

Deep Humiliation of Soul

Secondly, in the centurion we see coupled with this high and noble repute, DEEP HUMILIATION OF SOUL. "I am not worthy that thou shouldest come under my roof."

Humility, then, it appears, may exist in any condition. There are some men who are too mean to be humble. Do you understand me? They are too crouching, crawling, sneakish, and abject to be humble. When they use humble words, they disgrace the words they use. You perceive at once that it is rather a rise than a stoop for them to be humble. How could it be otherwise? It certainly is not for the least vermin that creep the earth to talk about humility. They must be low: it is their proper place. Such the creatures who cringe and fawn—"Whatever you please, sir"; "Yes"; "No"; in the same breath. They have not a soul within them that would be worth the notice of a sparrow-hawk. They are too little to be worthy of observation, yet they say they are humble. But a man to be humble, needs to have a soul: to stoop, you must have some elevation to stoop from; you must have some real excellence within you before you can really understand what it is to renounce merit. Had he been unworthy, had he been ungenerous and an oppressor, he would have spoken the truth when he said, "I am not worthy that thou shouldest come under my roof"; but there would have been no true humility in what he said. It was because of his excellence, as acknowledged by others, that he could be humble in the modesty of his opinion of himself. We have heard of a certain monk, who, professing to be humble, said he had broken all God's commandments; he was the greatest sinner in the world; he was as bad as Judas. Somebody said, "Why tell us that? We have all of us thought that a long time!" Straightway the holy man grew red in the face, and smote the accuser, and asked him what he had ever done to deserve such a speech. We know some of that kind: they will use the words of humility; appear very contrite; and perhaps even at prayer meetings you would think them the meekest and most brokenhearted of men; but if you were to take them at their word, straightway they would tell you they use the language, as some ecclesiastical personages do, in a non-natural sense; they do not quite mean what they were supposed to mean, but something very different. That is not humility: it is a kind of mock-modesty which hankers after applause, and holds out specious words as a bait for the trap of approbation. Our centurion was truly humble. This a man may be, though possessing the highest excellence, and standing in the most eminent position. I believe, in my soul, that no man had truer humility in him than John Knox, and yet John Knox never cringes, and never bows. When Luther dared the thunders of the Vatican, no doubt many said how self-conceited, egotistical, and proud he was; but for all that, God knew how humbly Martin Luther walked with him. When Athanasius stood up, and said, "I, Athanasius, against the world," it had the ring of pride about, but there was true and sound humility before God in it, because he seemed to say, "What am I? not worthy of taking care of; and therefore I do not use the subterfuges of cowardice for my own personal safety; let the world do what it will to me, God's truth is infinitely more precious than I am, and so I give myself up as an offering upon its altar." True humility will comport with the highest chivalry in maintaining divine truth, and with the boldest assertion of what one knows in his own conscience to be true. Though it may be the lot of Christians to be *thought* proud, let it never be true or capable of being substantiated concerning them.

The centurion, though worthy, was still humble; his friends and neighbors found him out by what he said and what he did. He asked them to go for him, seeing he was not worthy; then, finding that they asked too great a boon, he comes to stop them: "I am not worthy that thou shouldest come under my roof." You need not tell people that you are humble. You have no occasion to advertise that you have genuine humility: let it discover itself as spice does, by its perfume: or as fire, by its burning. If you live near to God, and if your humility is of the right kind, it will tell its own tale ere long. But the place where humility does speak out, is at the throne of grace. Beloved, there are some things we would confess of ourselves before God, which we would not confess before men. There is an attitude of prostration at the throne of the Most High, which will never be so gracefully or graciously taken as by that man who would spurn to prostrate himself before his fellows. That is no true humility which bends the knee at the tyrant's throne: that is true humility which, having bearded the tyrant to his face, goes down on its knees before the God of heaven: bold as a lion before men, but meek as a lamb before Jehovah. The true man, whom God approves, will not, dares not swerve, for the love he bears his sovereign Lord, when he faces men; but when he is alone with his Maker, he veils his face with something better than the wings of angels. Wrapped all over with the blood and righteousness of Jesus Christ, he rejoices with fear and trembling that he is justified from all things now; yet, conscious of the total defilement of his nature, with deep prostration of soul he uses the leper's cry, "Unclean! unclean! unclean!" Thus does he fix all his hope upon that cleansing blood, and depend alone on that meritorious obedience of Jesus, upon which every sanctified believer exclusively relies. Seek, then, as much as lies in you, that high character which the Christian should maintain among men; but with it always blend that true humility which comes of the Spirit of God, and ever behooves us in the presence of the Lord.

We Should Never Diminish Our Faith in God

The main thing I am aiming at, because, after all, the most practical, lies in my third point. However deep our humility, however conscious we may be of our own undeservingness, WE SHOULD NEVER DIMINISH OUR FAITH IN GOD.

Observe the confession: "I am not worthy that thou shouldest come under my roof." What then will be the inference? "I fear, therefore, my servant will not be healed"? No, no; but—"Say in a word, and my servant shall be healed." It is all a mistake that great faith implies pride. Beloved, the greater faith, the deeper humility. These are brothers, not foes. The more the glories of God strike your eyes, the humbler you will be in conscious abasement, but yet the higher you will rise in importunate prayer. Let us take this principle, and endeavor to apply it to a few cases. I say that a deep sense of our own nothingness is not to prevent our having strong faith. We will take a few instances.

There is a minister here who has been preaching the Word of God: he has so proclaimed it that God has been pleased to own it in some degree; but, it may be, he has stirred up strife; he has caused I know not what amount of turmoil and of noise, as the faithful servant of God will in his measure; and now, coming before God, he is asking that a greater blessing than ever may rest upon his labors; but something checks his tongue. He remembers his many infirmities; he recollects, perhaps, how slack he is in his private devotions, and how cold he is in his pleading with the sons of men. He has before him the promise, "My word shall not return unto me void"; but for all that, so conscious is he that he does not deserve the honor of being useful, that he is half afraid to pray as he should pray, and to believe as he should believe. Dear brother, may I press upon you the case of the centurion? It is right for you, it is right for me, to say, "Lord, I am not worthy to be made the spiritual parent of one immortal soul." It is right for me to feel that it is too great an honor to be permitted to preach the truth at all, and almost too high a thing for such a sinner to have any jewels to present to the Redeemer to fix in His crown; but, oh! we must not from this infer that He will not fulfill His promise to us, and hear our prayer, "Lord, speak in a word, and, feeble though the instrument may be, the congregation shall be blessed: say but the word, and the marvelous testimony, though marred with a thousand imperfections, shall yet be 'quick and powerful, and sharper than any two-edged sword.'" Let this comfort and cheer any desponding pastor: let him take heart from this, and learn that it is not himself to whom he is to look to, but that he is to look to God;

and that it is not his own arm upon which he is to depend, but the promise of God and the strong arm of the Most High. Or, am I addressing some brother or sister in somewhat similar perplexity of mind? In your private life, dear friend, you have laid upon your heart some of your relatives and neighbors who are very dear to you; or, perhaps, you teach a class in Sunday school, or possibly you have a larger class of adults, and sometimes Satan will be very busy with you. The more useful you are, the more busy he will be; and he will say to you, "What are you, that you should ever hope to see conversions? Other men and women have had them, but they were better than you are: they had more talent; they had more ability; they served God better; and God gave them a greater reward. You must not hope to see your children saved; you cannot expect it. How should such teaching as yours ever be useful?" Friend, you are right in saying, "Lord, I am not worthy that thou shouldest come under my roof." The more you can feel *that*, the more hopeful shall I be of your success. You are right in feeling that David is not fit to meet the giant, and that the stones out of the brook are scarcely fit weapons for such a warfare; but, oh! do not push the right into a wrong; do not, therefore, mistrust your God. No matter what a fool you may be: God has confounded wise things by the foolish, long ere now. No matter how weak you are: God has brought down the mighty by weak instrumentalities often enough before this time. Have you hope in Him; and tonight in your prayer, when you have made your confessions, do not let your faith fail you, but say, "Lord, say in a word, and my class shall be blessed; say in a word, and those stubborn boys and girls, those to whom I have talked so often, who seem to be none the better, shall be saved." Have faith in God, beloved fellow-workers! The result of all, under God, must rest with your faith. If you believe for *little* success, you shall have little success; but if you can believe for *great* things, and expect great things, you shall certainly find your Master's words fulfilling your desire. Do I now also address parents here who have been praying for their children? or a husband who has been pleading for his wife? or a wife who has been making intercession for her husband? God only knows what heart-rending prayers are often heard in families where only a part is saved! Ah! what grief is it to a truly godly father to see his sons and daughters still heirs of wrath! And what a pang to know that the partner of your bosom must be separated from you forever by the stroke of death! I marvel not that you pray for your friends. Should I not marvel at you if you did not? And now, when you have been praying lately, a sense of your unworthiness has almost stopped you; and though, perhaps, there has been no public sin about you; though before others you could have defended yourself, you have said in private, "Lord, I am not worthy of this blessing." You have said, "Lord, my children are not saved, because my example is not as good as it should be; my conversation is not as upright as it should be." You have felt, as I have sometimes, that there was no creature in the whole world so little, and no man loved of God in all the world that was so great a wonder of ingratitude as you are. I say it is right that you should feel this, but do not let this stop your prayers; proffer your request; depend upon the blood of Christ for its plea, and upon the intercession of Christ for its prevalence. Do not be afraid. A black hand drops a letter into the post-office, but the blackness of that hand will not hinder the despatch of it; there is a stamp upon it, and it will go. And your black hand drops a prayer before Christ's feet, but that black hand will not stop its being heard, for there is a stamp upon it—Jehovah Jesus' blood. It may be blotted and mis-spelled, and there may be many blurs all over it; but do not be afraid, for God knows His Son's signature, and that will give a worth to your prayers. It is the bloody signature of Him whose hand was nailed to the cross that will carry the day with God. Therefore do not, I pray you, give place to fear; your prayers shall return into your bosom with an answer of peace.

"Well, but," says one, "I have prayed so long." Ah! brother, do not "limit the Holy One of Israel." Sister, do not let your doubts prevail. Renew your appeal to Jesus, "Say in a word: only say one word." It is all done if He shall speak. Darkness fled before Him in the primeval chaos, and order followed confusion. Think you, if He shall say, "Let there be light," in a dark heart, that there shall not be light there? Angels fly at His bidding: at His presence the rocks melt, and the hills dissolve: Sinai is altogether on a smoke; and when He comes forth, dressed in the robes of salvation, there are no impossibilities with Him. He can win and conquer to your heart's best desire. Therefore be humble, but be not unbelieving.

By your leave, I shall now turn the principle of my text to an account in another way. Concerning yourselves, friends, what are the mercies which you want? If every man could write down his own peculiar prayer, what a variety we should have upon the paper as it just went around the front row of that gallery. If it went around to all, it would not be like Jeremiah's roll, written within and without with lamentations, but it would be filled within and without with divers' petitions. But now just imagine what your own case is, and the case of others, and let us apply this prin-ciple to it: we are utterly unworthy to obtain the temporal or spiritual mercy which, it may be, we are now seeking: we may feel this, but in asking any-thing for ourselves, we must still ask in faith in God, in His promise, and in His grace; and we shall prevail. This blessed principle may be turned to all sorts of uses. Whatever your desire may be, only believe, and it shall be granted unto you if it be a desire in accordance with His will, and in accor-dance with the promises of His Word; or else God's Word is not true. Be humble about it, but do not be doubtful about it. The case I have in my mind's eye, is this: there is an unsaved soul here tonight. It happens to be one whose character has been morally admirable, Nobody finds any fault with you; and, as I said before, you almost wish they could; for you cannot feel, as some do, the terrors of the Lord, Your heart is not broken with conviction as the hearts of some are, but there is this desire in it, "Lord, save me, or I perish!" Now, dear friend, it is well that you should feel that there is nothing in you to commend you to Christ. I am glad that you do feel this. Though before the eyes of men, and even of your own parents, there is nothing which can cause you a blush, I am glad that you feel that before God you have nothing whatever to boast of. I think I see you now: you are saying, "My church-goings, my chapel-goings, I do not trust in *them.* I would not give up attendance at the means of grace, but, sir, I have no reliance upon all this. As for my baptism, or my confirmation, or my taking the sacrament, I know that all this has nothing whatever in it which can save my soul; and though I *love* God's ordinances, yet I cannot *trust* in them. Sir, I have fed the poor; I have taught the ignorant. In my measure I would do anything to assist those who need my aid; but I do solemnly renounce all this as a ground of trust. Nothing have I of which to glory."

Well now, dear friend, there remains only one thing to give you perfect peace tonight; and may the Master give you that one thing! Lift up this prayer to Him, "Say in a word, and I shall be made whole." Christ can do it; the offering is made; the precious blood is spilt; there is an almighty efficacy in it: He *can* put away your sin. Christ lives to intercede before the throne, and "is able also to save them to the uttermost that come unto God by him." Doubt not, then, but now, trusting yourself with Jesus Christ, remember you are saved. I am not now looking after the vilest of the vile. How many times have we said from this place that none are excluded hence but those who do themselves exclude. No mountains of sin, nor height of vileness, can shut a man out of heaven if he believes in Jesus; but just now we are after *you.* I know you are a numerous class. You are, in some respects, our dear friends; and though not of us, you hover around us. If there is anything to be done for the cause of God, you are, perhaps, first in it; and yet you yourselves are not saved. I cannot bear the thought of your being cast away—to be so near the gates of heaven, and yet to be shut out after all. Why should it be? The voice speaks to you now: the spirit of the living God speaks through that voice. There is life in a look for *you* as well as for the chief of sinners. Without the strong convictions, without the terrors of conscience, without a sense of any aggravated crimes, if you rest on Jesus, you are saved. There is no amount of sin specified there. You are lost in the fall—wholly lost, even if you had no sin of your own; but your own actual sin has irretrievably ruined you apart from the grace of Christ. You know this, and to an extent you feel it. You will feel it all the more when you have believed in Jesus. But now the one message of mercy is, "Believe, and thou shalt live." I feel as if I cannot get at you. My soul will not go out as I can desire, and yet you know that I am thinking about you and about your case. When we are firing our shots at sin, we hardly ever strike you. You have become so used to our appeals that there seems no likelihood of our getting at you. Or! there are some of you whom I would not find fault with if I could. You make your brother glad with your industry; you make your sister's heart rejoice at your many virtues; but yet there is *one thing* which you lack. Remember that when the strength of a chain is to be measured, it is measured at its one weakest link. If you have that one weak link the vital union is snapped. You may have anything and everything else, but you will be only a child of nature and not a living son. I am only telling you over and over truths which you have known for many years. You will not dispute these things; and sometimes you feel an earnestness about your eternal portion, though, like so many others, you are putting off and putting off. But death will not put off; the judgment day will not be postponed for you. O may you be now brought in! What a happy church we should be if such as you should be brought in. We rejoice over the chief of sinners; we make the place ring when the prodigals come in; but elder brother, why will not you come in—you who have not been standing all the day idle in the market, but only the first hour; say not, no man has hired you. O come in, that the house of mercy may be filled! God grant the desire of our hearts, and to His name shall be the praise. Amen and Amen.

8

*The Prodigal's Reception**

*And he arose, and came to his father. But when he was yet a great
way off his father saw him, and had compassion, and ran, and fell
on his neck, and kissed him (Luke 15:20).*

There he is! He is as wretched as misery itself; as filthy as his brute associates who could satisfy themselves with husks, while he could not. His clothes hang about him in rags, and what he is without, that he is within. He is disgraced in the eyes of the good, and the virtuous remember him with indignation. He has some desires to go back to his father's house; but *these desires are not sufficient to alter his condition.* Mere desires have not scraped the filth from him, nor have they so much as shed his rags. Whatever he may or may not desire, he is still filthy, still disgraced, still an alien from his father's house: and he knows it, for he has come to himself. He would have been angry if we had said as much as this before, but now we cannot describe him in words too black. With many tears and sighs he assures us that he is even worse than he appears to be, and that no man can know all the depth of the vileness of his conduct: he has spent his living with harlots; he has despised a generous parent's love and broken loose from his wise control; he has done evil with both his hands to the utmost of his strength and opportunity. There he stands, notwithstanding this confession, just what I have described him to be; for even though he has said within himself "I have sinned," yet *that confession has not removed his griefs.* He acknowledges that he is not worthy to be called a son—and it is true he is not; but his unworthiness is not removed by his consciousness of it, nor by his confession of it. He has no claims to a father's love. If that father shuts the door in his face, he acts with justice to him; if he shall refuse so much as to speak a single word, except words of rebuke, no one can blame the father, for the son has so sadly erred. To

---

* This sermon is taken from *The Metropolitan Tabernacle Pulpit* and was preached on Sunday morning, September 4, 1864.

94

this the son utters no demur; he confesses that if he be cast away forever, he deserves it well. This picture, I know, is the photograph of some who are now present. You feel your vileness and sinfulness, but you cannot look upon that sense of vileness as in any way extenuating or altering your condition. You feel, but you cannot plead your feelings. You confess this morning that you have desires toward God, but that you have no rights to Him—you cannot demand anything at His hands. If your soul were sent to hell, His righteous law approves it, and so does your own conscience. You can see your rags, you can mark your filthiness, you can long for something better, but you *are* no better; you have no more claims than you used to have upon God's mercy; you stand here today, a self-convicted offender against the lovingkindness and holiness of God. I pray that to such of you as are in this case, I may be the bearer of a message from God to your soul this morning. O you who know the Lord, put up earnest and silent prayers just now, that my message may come home with power to troubled consciences; and I beseech you, for your own profit, look back to the hole of the pit whence you were digging, and to the miry clay whence you were drawn, and remember how God received you. And while we talk of what He is willing and able do to the far off sinners, let your souls leap with joyous gratitude at the recollection of how He received you into His love, and made you takers of his grace in days gone by.

There are two things in the text: the first is *the condition of many a seeker—he is yet a great way off*; and then, secondly, *the matchless kindness of the Father toward him.*

The Condition of Such a Seeker—He Is Yet a Great Way Off

First, dear friends, THE CONDITION OF SUCH A SEEKER—HE IS YET A GREAT WAY OFF. He is a great way off if you consider one or two things. Remember *his want of strength*. This poor young man had for some time been without food—brought so very low that the husks upon which the swine fed would have seemed a dainty to him if he could have eaten them. He is so hungry that he has become emaciated, and to him every mile has the weariness of leagues within it. It costs him many pains and sore griefs to drag himself along, even though it be but an inch. So the sinner is a long way off from God when you consider his utter want of strength to come to God. Even such strength as God has given him is very painfully used. God has given him strength enough to desire salvation, but those desires are always accompanied with deep and sincere grief for sin. The point which he has already reached has exhausted all his power, and all he can do is to fall down before Jesus, and say,

> Oh! for this no strength have I,
> My strength is at thy feet to lie.

He is a great way off again, if you consider *his want of courage.* He longs to see his father, but yet the probabilities are that if his father should come he would run away: the very sound of his father's footsteps would act upon him as they did on Adam in the garden—he would hide himself among the trees; so that instead of crying after his father, the great Father would have to cry after him—"Where art thou, poor fallen creature? where art thou?" His want of courage, therefore, makes the distance long, for every step hitherto has been taken as though into the jaws of death. "Ah!" said the sinner, "it must be long before I can dare to hope, for mine iniquities have gone over my head so that I cannot look up." Are you then in alarm and dread this morning? Your prayers seem to yourself to have been no prayers at all; when you think of God, terror comes over your mind, and you feel that you are a long, long way from Him; you imagine that it is not likely that He will hear your cries nor give heed to your words. You are yet a great way off.

You are a great way off when we consider *the difficulty of the way of repentance.* John Bunyan tells us that Christian found, when he went back to the arbor after his lost roll, that it was very hard work going back. Every backslider finds it so, and every penitent sinner knows that there is a bitterness in mourning for sin comparable to the loss of one's only son. A drowning man feels no great pain: the sensations of drowning are even said to be pleasant; it is only when the man is being restored to life, when the blood begins to make the veins tingle because life leaps there, when once again the nerves are sensible, then we are told that the whole body is full of many agonies, but then they are the agonies of life: and so the poor penitent feels the goal must be a great way, for if he had to feel as he now feels, even for a month, it were a great time; and if he had to journey many miles as he now journeys, so painfully, with such bleeding feet, it would indeed be a great way.

Let us look into this matter, and show that while the road seems long on this account, *it really is long* if we view it in certain lights. There are many seeking sinners who are a great way off in *their life.* I think I see the man now, and hear him thus bewail himself, "I have left off my drunkenness. I could not sit where I used to sit by the hour. I thank God I shall never be seen reeling through the streets again, for that groveling lust I detest. I have given up Sabbath-breaking, and I am found in God's house; and I have endeavored, as much as I can, to renounce the habit of swearing, but still I am a great way off; I do not feel as if I could yet lay hold of Christ, for I cannot master my own passions yet. An old companion stopped me this week, and he had not long been talking before I found the old man was in me, and the old lustings came up into my face again. Why, sir, the other day an oath came rapping out. I thought I had got over it, but I had not— I am a great way off. When I read of what saints are, and observe what true

Christians are, I do feel that my conduct is so inconsistent and so widely apart from what it ought to be, that I am a great way off. Ah! dear friend, you are; and if you had to come to God by the way of your own right-eousness you would never reach Him, for He is not thus to be found. Christ Jesus is the way. He is the safe, sure, and perfect road to God. He who sees Jesus, has seen the Father; but he who looks to himself will only see despair. The road to heaven by Mount Sinai is impassable by mortal man, but Calvary leads to glory; the secret places of the stairs are in the wounds of Jesus.

Again, you feel yourself a great way off as to *knowledge*. "Why," say you, "before I felt thus I considered myself a master of all theology: I could twist the doctrines around my fingers. When I listened to a sermon I felt quite able to criticize it, and to give my judgment. Now I see that my judg-ment was about as valuable as the criticism of a blind man upon a picture, for I was without spiritual sight. Now I feel myself to be a fool. I do know what sin means, but only to a degree. Even here I feel that I am not con-scious of the heinousness of human guilt. I have heard the doctrine of the atonement of Christ, and I thank God I know it to some degree, but the excellence and glory of the substitutionary sacrifice which Christ offered I confess I do not fully comprehend." The sinner's confession now is that instead of understanding Scripture he finds he needs to go like a child to school to learn the A B C of it. "O sir," says he, "I am a great way off from God, for I am so ignorant, so foolish, I seem to be but as a beast when I think of the deep things of God." Ah! poor soul, poor young wandering brother, I wonder not that it seems so to you, for the ignorance of the car-nal man is indeed fearful, and only God can give you light; but he can give it to you in a moment, and the distance between you and Him upon the score of ignorance can be bridged at once, and you may comprehend even today, with all saints, what are the heights and depths, and know the love of Christ which passes knowledge.

In another point also many an earnest seeker is a great way off, I mean in *his repentance*. "Alas!" says he, "I cannot repent as I ought. If I could feel the brokenness of heart which I have heard and seen in some! Oh! what would I give for penitential sighs; how thankful should I be if my head were waters, and mine eyes fountains of tears, if I could even feel that I was as humble as the poor publican, and could stand with downcast eyes and beat upon my breast and say, 'God be merciful to me a sinner.' But, alas! I have been a hearer of the Word for years, and all the progress I have made is so little, that while I know the gospel to be true, I do not feel it. I know myself to be a sinner, and sometimes I mourn over it, but my mourn-ing is so superficial, my repentance is a repentance that needs to be repented of. O sir, if God would use the heaviest hammer that He had, if He would but break my heart, every broken fragment should bless His name. I wish I had a genuine repentance. Oh! how I pant to be brought to feel that I am lost, and to desire Christ with that vehement desire which will not take a denial; but in this point my heart seems hard as hell-hardened steel, cold as a rock of ice, it will not, cannot yield, though wooed by love divine. Adamant itself may run in liquid torrents, but my soul yields to nothing. Lord, break it! Lord, break it!!" Ah! poor heart, I see you are a great way off, but do you know if my Lord should appear to you this morning, and say to you, "I have loved you with an everlasting love," your heart would break in a moment?

> Law and terrors do but harden,
>   All the while they work alone;
> But a sense of blood-bought pardon,
>   Can dissolve a heart of stone.

Great way off as you are, if the Lord pardons you, while yet callous, and consciously hard of heart, will you not then fall at His feet and commend that great love wherewith He loved you, even when you were dead in trespasses and sins?

Yes, but I think I hear one say, "There is another point in which I feel a great way off, for I have little or no *faith*. I have heard faith preached every Sabbath day; I know what it is, I think I do, but I cannot reach it. I know that if I cast myself wholly upon Christ I shall be saved. I quite comprehend that He does not ask anything of me, any willings, or doings, or feelings: I know that Christ is willing to receive the greatest sinner out of hell if that sinner will but come and simply trust Him. I have tried to do it; sometimes I have thought I had faith, but then again when I have looked at my sins I have doubted so dreadfully, that I perceive I have no faith at all. There are sunshiny moments with me when I think I can say—

> My faith is built on nothing less,
> Than Jesus' blood and righteousness.

But oh! when I feel my corruptions within rising upon me, I hear a voice saying, "The Philistines be upon thee, Samson," and straightway I discover my own weakness. I have not the faith that I want; I am a great way off from it, and I fear that I shall never possess it. Yes, my brethren, I perceive your difficulty, for I have felt the sorrow of it myself; but oh! my Lord, who is the Giver of faith, who is exalted on high to give repentance and remission of sins, can give you the faith you so much desire, and can cause you this morning to rest with perfect confidence upon the work which He has finished for you.

To gather up all things in one word, the truly penitent sinner feels that he is yet a great way off *in everything*. There is no point upon which you can talk with him but it will be sure to lead to a confession of his deficiency. Begin to put him in the scales of the sanctuary, and he cries, "Alas! before you put in the weights I can tell you I shall be found wanting." Bring him to the touchstone, and he shrinks from it; "Nay," says he, "but I cannot endure any sort of trial—

> All unholy and unclean,
> I am nothing else but sin."

See, see, how well my Master has pictured your case in this parable— "Yet a great way off," yet covered with rags, yet polluted with filth, yet in disgrace, yet a stranger to your Father's house, there is only this one point about you, you have your face toward your Father, you have a desire toward God, and you would, oh! you would if you could, lay hold upon eternal life. But you feel too far off for anything like comfortable hope; now I must confess I feel many fears about you who are in this state; I am afraid lest you should come so far and yet go back; for there are many whom we thought had come as far as this, and yet they have gone back after all. Oh! remember that desires after God will not change you so as to save you. You must find Christ. Remember that to say, "I will arise" is not enough, nor even to arise; you must never rest till your Father has given you the kiss, till He has put on you the best robe. I am afraid lest you should rest satisfied and say, "I am in a good state; the minister tells us that many are brought to such a state before they are saved. I will stop here." My dear friend, it is a good state *to pass through*, but it is a bad state *to rest in*. I pray you never be content with a sense of sin, never be satisfied with merely knowing that you are not what you ought to be. It never cures the fever for a man to know he has it; his knowledge is in some degree a good sign, for it proves that fever has not yet driven him to delirium; but it never gives a perfect health to know that he is sick. It is a good thing for him to know it, for he will not otherwise send for the physician; but except lead to that, he will die whether he feels himself to be sick or no. A mere consciousness that you are hungry while your father's hired servants have bread enough and to spare, will not stay your hunger, you want more than this. You are a great way off, and I beseech you remember the danger is, lest you should stop here or should lose what sensibility you already have. Perhaps despair may come upon you. Some have committed suicide while under a sense of the greatness of their distance from God, because they dared not look to the Savior. Our prayers shall go up to God that the second part of our text may come true to you, and that alike backsliding and despair may be prevented by the speedy coming of God dressed in the robes of grace to meet your guilty soul, and give you joy and peace through believing.

The Matchless Kindness of the Heavenly Father

Secondly—and O may the Master give us His help—we have to consider THE MATCHLESS KINDNESS OF THE HEAVENLY FATHER. We must take each word and dwell upon it.

First of all, we have here *divine observation.* "When he was yet a great way off *his father saw him.*" It is true he has always seen him. God sees the sinner in every state and in every position. Ay, and sees him with an eye of love too—such a chosen sinner as is described in this text—not with complacency, but still with affection. God looks upon His wandering chosen ones. I say that father saw his son when he spent his living with harlots, saw him with deep sorrow, when he fain would have filled his belly with the husks which the swine did eat; but now, if there can be such a thing as for divine omniscience to become more exact, the father sees him with an eye full of a more tender love, a greater care. "His father saw *him.*" Oh! what a sight it was for a father to see! His son, it is true, but his reprobate son, who had dishonored his father's name; brought down the name of an honorable house to be mentioned among the dregs and scum of the earth. There he is! What a sight for a *father's* eye! He is filthy, as though he had been rolling in the mire; and his beautiful clothing has long ago lost its fine colors, and hangs about him in wretched rags. The father does not turn away and try to forget him, he fixes his full gaze upon him. Sinner, you know that God sees you this morning; sitting in this house you are observed of the God of heaven. There is not a desire in your heart unread of Him, nor a tear in your eye which He does not observe. I tell you He has seen your midnight sins, He has heard your cursings and your blasphemies, and yet He has loved you notwithstanding all that you have done. You could hardly have been a worse rebel against Him, and yet He has noted you in His book of love, and determined to save you, and the eye of His love has followed you whithersoever you have gone. Is there not some comfort here? Why could not *he* see his father? Was it the effect of the tears in his eyes that he could not see? or was it that his father was of quicker sight than he? Sinner, you cannot see God, you are unbelieving, and carnal, and blind, but He can see you; your tears of penitence block up your sight, but your Father is quick of eye, and He beholds you and loves you now; in every glance there is love. "His father saw him."

Observe this was a loving observation, for it is written, "*His father* saw him." He did not see him as a mere casual observer; he did not note him as a man might note his friend's child with some pity and benevolence, but he marked him as a father alone can do. What a quick eye a parent has! Why, I have known a young man come home, perhaps for a short holiday: the mother has heard nothing, not even a whisper, as to her son's conduct, and yet she cannot help observing to her husband, "There is a something about John which makes me suspect that he is not going on as

he should do. I do not know, my husband," she says, "what it is, but yet
I am sure he is getting among bad companions." She will read his character at once. And the father notes something, too, he cannot precisely say
what, but cause for anxiety he knows it to be. But here we have a Father
who can see everything, and who has as much of the quickness of love as
he has of the certainty of knowledge. He can, therefore, see from every
spot and bruise, and note every putrefying sore. He sees His poor son right
through as though he were a vase of crystal; He reads his heart, not merely the tell-tale garments, not merely the sorrowful tale of the unwashed
face and those clouted shoes, but He can read his soul, He understands the
whole of his miserable plight. O poor sinner, there is no need for you to
give information to your God, for He knows it already; you need not pick
your words in prayer in order to make your case plain and perspicuous,
for God can see it, and all you have to do is to uncover your wounds, your
bruises, and your putrefying sores, and say, "My Father, thou seest it all,
the black tale thou readest in a moment, my Father, have pity upon me."

The next thought to be well considered is *divine compassion.* "When he
saw him he had compassion on him." Does not the word *com-passion*
meaning *suffering-with* or *fellow-suffering*? What is compassion, then, but
putting yourself into the place of the sufferer and feeling his grief? If I may
so say, the father put himself into the son's rags, and then felt as much pity
for him as that poor ragged prodigal could have felt for himself. I do not
know how to bring up your compassion this morning, except it is by sup-
posing that it is your own case. I will suppose, father, it is a son of yours.
I saw, not many hours ago, a young man who brought to my mind the
prodigal in this case: his face marked with innumerable lines of sin and
wretchedness, his body lean and emaciated, his clothes close-buttoned, his
whole appearance the very mirror of woe. He knocked at my door. I knew
his case; I cannot hurt him by telling it. He had disgraced his family, not
once nor twice, but many times. At last he drew out what money he had in
the business of respectable family, came up to London with four hundred
pounds, and in about five weeks spent it all; and, without a single farthing
to help himself he often wants for bread, and I fear that he has often crept
at night into the parks to sleep, and thus has brought aches and pains into
his bones which will hold by him till he dies. He wanders the streets by a
day a vagabond and a reprobate. I have written to his friends, the case has
been put before them; they will not own him; and considering his shameful conduct, I do not wonder at it. He has no father and no mother left. If he
were helped beyond mere food and lodging, as far as we can judge, it would
be money thrown away; if he were helped, he seems so desperately set on
wickedness, that he would do the same again. Yet as I think, I can but desire
to see him have one more trial at the least, and he would have it, I doubt not,
if *his father* yet lived; but others feel the fountains of their love are stayed.

As I think of him, I cannot but feel that if he were a son of mine and I were his father, and I saw him in such a case come to my door, whatever the crime was that he had committed, I must fall upon his neck and kiss him; the most huge sin could not put out forever the sparks of paternal love. I might condemn the sin in terms the sharpest and most severe; I might regret that he had ever been born, and cry with David, "O my son Absalom, my son, my son Absalom! would God I had died for thee!" but I could not shut him out of my house, nor refuse to call him my child. My child he is, and my child he shall be till he dies. You feel just now that if it were your child you would do the same. That is how God feels toward you, His chosen, His repentant child. You *are* His child; I hope so, I trust so; those desires which you have in your soul toward Him, make me feel that you are one of His children, and as God looks out of heaven He knows what you mean. What is it? What shall I say? Nay, I need not describe, but, "Like as a father pitieth his children, so the Lord pitieth them that fear him." He will have compassion upon you; He will receive you to His bosom now. Be of good courage, for the text says, "He had compassion on him."

Notice and observe carefully *the swiftness of this divine love*: "He ran." Probably he was walking on the top of his house and looking out for his son, when one morning he just caught a glimpse of a poor sorry figure in the distance. If he had been anything but the father he would not have known it to be his son, he was so altered; but he looked and looked again, till at last he said, "It is he! oh! what marks of famine are upon him, and of suffering too!" And down comes the old gentleman—I think I see him running downstairs, and the servants come to the windows and the doors, and say, "Where is master going? I have not seen him run at that rate for many a-day." See, there he goes; he does not take the road, for that is a little round about; but there is a gap through the hedge, and he is jumping over it; the straightest way that he can find he chooses; and before the son has had time to notice who it is, he is on him, and has his arms about him, falling upon his neck and kissing him. I recollect a young prodigal who was received in the same way. Here he stands, it is I, myself. I sat in a little chapel, little dreaming that *my Father* saw me; certainly I was a great way off. I felt something of my need of Christ, but I did not know what I must do to be saved; though taught the letter of the Word, I was spiritually ignorant of the plan of salvation; though taught it from my youth up, I knew it not. I felt, but I did not feel what I wished to feel. If ever there was a soul that knew itself to be far off from God, I was that soul; and yet in a moment, in one single moment, no sooner had I heard the words, "Look unto me and be ye saved, all the ends of the earth," no sooner had I turned my eyes to Jesus crucified, than I felt my perfect reconciliation with God, I knew my sins to be forgiven. There was no time for getting out of my heavenly Father's way, it was done, and done in an instant; and in my case, at least, He ran and fell upon my neck to kiss me. I hope that will be the case this morning; before you can get out of this place, before you can get back to your old doubtings, and fearings, and sighings, and cryings, I hope here the Lord of love will run and meet you, and fall upon your neck and kiss you.

After noticing thus, *observation, compassion,* and *swiftness,* do not forget *the nearness*: "He fell upon his neck and kissed him." This I can understand by experience, but it is too wonderful for me to explain, "he fell upon his neck." If he had stood at a distance and said, "John, I should be very glad to kiss you, but you are too filthy; I do not know what may be under those filthy rags: I do not feel inclined to fall upon your neck just yet; you are too far gone for me. I love you, but there is a limit to the display of love. When I have got you into a proper state, then I may manifest my affection to you, but I cannot just now, while you are so very foul." Oh! no; but before he is washed he falls on his neck—there is the wonder of it. I can understand how God manifests His love to a soul that is washed in Jesus' blood, and know it; but how He could fall upon the neck of a foul, filthy sinner *as such!* There it is—not as sanctified, not as having anything good in himself, but as nothing but a filthy, foul, desperate rebel, God falls upon his neck and kisses him. Oh! strange miracle of love! The riddle is unriddled when you recollect that God never had looked upon that sinner, as he was in himself, but had always looked upon him as he was in Christ; and when He fell upon that prodigal's neck, He did in effect only fall upon the neck of His once-suffering Son, Jesus Christ, and He kissed the sinner because He saw him in Christ, and therefore did not see the sinner's loathsomeness, but saw only Christ's comeliness, and therefore kissed him as He would have kissed his substitute. Observe how near God comes to the sinner. It was said of that eminent saint and martyr, Bishop Hooper, that on one occasion a man in distress was allowed to go into his prison to tell his tale of conscience; but Bishop Hooper looked so sternly upon him, and addressed him so severely at first, that the poor soul ran away, and could not get comfort until he had sought out another minister of a gentler aspect. Now Hooper really was a gracious and loving soul, but the sternness of his manner kept the penitent off. There is no such stern manner in our heavenly Father, He loves to receive His prodigals. When He comes there is no "Hold off!" no " Keep off!" to the sinner, but He falls upon his neck and He kisses him.

There is yet another thought to be brought out of the metaphor of kissing; we are not to pass that over without dipping our cup in the honey. In kissing his son the father *recognizes relationship*. He said, with emphasis, "Thou art my son," and the prodigal was

> To his Father's bosom pressed,
> Once for all a child confessed.

Again, that kiss was the seal of *forgiveness*. He would not have kissed him if he had been angry with him; he forgave him, forgave him all. There was, moreover, something more than forgiveness, there was *acceptance*—"I receive you back into my heart as though you were worthy of all that I give to your elder brother, and therefore I kiss you." Surely also this was a kiss of delight—as if he took pleasure in him, delighting in him, feasting his eyes with the sight of him, and feeling more happy to see him than to see all his fields, and the fatted calves, and the treasures that he possessed. His delight was in seeing this poor restored child. Surely this is all summed up in a kiss. And if this morning my Father, and your Father, should come out to meet mourning penitents, in a moment He will show you that you are His children, you shall say, "Abba, Father," on your road to your own house; you shall feel that your sin is all forgiven, that every particle of it is cast behind Jehovah's back; you shall feel today that you are accepted as your faith looks to Christ you shall see that God accepts you, because Christ your substitute is worthy of God's love and God's delight. Nay; I trust you shall this very morning delight yourself in God, because God delights Himself in you, and you shall hear Him whisper in your ear, "Thou shalt be called Hephzibah . . . for the Lord delighteth in thee." I wish I could picture such a text as this as it ought to be; it needs some tender, sympathetic heart, some man who is the very soul of pathos, to work out the tender touches of such a verse as this. But, oh! though I cannot describe it, I hope you will feel it, and that is better than description. I come not here to paint the scene, except to be the brush in God's hand to paint it on your hearts. There are some of you who can say, "I do not want descriptions, for I have felt it; I went to Christ and told Him my case, and prayed Him to meet me; now I believe on Him, and I have gone my way rejoicing in Him."

We will just say these words and have done. In summing up, one may notice that this sinner, though he was a great way off, was *not received to full pardon and to adoption and acceptance by a gradual process, but he was received at once.* He was not allowed to enter into the outhouse first, and to sleep in a barn at night, and then afterward allowed to come sometimes and have his meals with the servants in the kitchen and then afterward allowed to sit at the bottom of the table and by degrees brought near. No; but the father fell on his neck and kissed him the first moment; he gets as near to God the first moment as he ever will. So a saved soul may not enjoy and know so much, but he is as near and dear to God the first moment he believes as he ever will be; a true heir of all things in Christ, and as truly so as even when he shall mount to heaven to be glorified and to be like his Lord. Oh! what a wonder is this? Fresh from his pigsty was he not, yet in a father's bosom; fresh from the swine with their gruntings in his ears, and now he bears a father's loving words; a few days ago he was putting husks to his mouth, and now it is a father's lips that are on his lips. What a change, and all at once. I say there is no gradual process in this, but the thing is done at once, in a moment he comes to his father, his father comes to him, and he is in his father's arms.

Observe again, as there was not a gradual reception, there was *not a partial reception*. He was not forgiven on conditions; he was not received to his father's heart if he would do so-and-so. No; there were no "ifs" and no "buts"; he was kissed, and clothed, and feasted, without a single condition of any kind whatever. No questions asked—his Father had cast his offenses behind his back in a moment, and he was received without even a censure or a rebuke. It was not a partial reception. He was not received to some things and refused others. He was not, for instance, allowed to call himself a child, but to think himself an inferior. No; he wears the best robe; he has the ring on his finger; he has the shoes on his feet; and he joins in eating the fatted calf; and so the sinner is not received to a second class place, but he is taken to the full position of a child of God. It is not a gradual nor yet a partial reception.

And once more, it is *not a temporary reception*. His father did not kiss him and then turn him out at the back door. He did not receive him for a time, and then afterward say to him, "Go your way; I have had pity upon you; you have now a new start, go into the far country and mend your ways." No; but the father would say to him what he had already said to the elder brother, "Son, thou art ever with me, and all that I have is thine." In the parable, the son could not have the goods restored, for he had spent his part; but in the truth itself and matter of fact, God does make the man who comes in at the eleventh hour equal with the one who came in at the first hour of the day; He gives every man the penny; and He gives to the child who has been the most wandering the same privileges, and ultimately the same heritage, which He gives to His own who have been these many years with Him, and have not transgressed His commandments. That is a remarkable passage in one of the prophets, where he says, "Ekron as a Jebusite"; meaning that the Philistine when converted should be treated just the same as the original inhabitants of Jerusalem; that the branches of the olive which were grafted in have the same privileges as the original branches. When God takes men from being heirs of wrath, and makes them heirs of grace, they have just as much privilege at the first as though they had been heirs of grace twenty years, because in God's sight they always were heirs of grace, and from all eternity He viewed His most wandering sons.

> Not as they stood in Adam's fall,
> When sin and ruin covered all;
> But as they'll stand another day,
> Fairer than sun's meridian ray.

O, I would to God that He would in His mercy bring some of His own dear children home this day—and He shall have the praise!

9

Our Lord's First Appearance Before Pilate *

Pilate saith unto them, I find in him no fault at all (John 18:38).

I should like, if God spares us, to present to you on Sunday mornings the full story of our Savior's sufferings. We began last Lord's day by going with Him to the hall of Caiaphas, and it was a sadly solemn time when we beheld the Prince of Peace a prisoner, heard Him falsely accused and unjustly condemned, and then saw Him abused, till servants and abjects did spit in His face and make a mockery of Him. I hope that you will not be wearied with this subject. If so, it will be the fault of the preacher, for the subject is ever full and fresh: or if the preacher be not to blame, there will be something of censure due to His hearers. If we do grow tired of the story of the cross it will be a sad indication of secret soul-sickness, and it will be well to observe the symptom and hasten to the great Physician for healing. To true saints in a healthy condition there is no place more attractive than the place of our Lord's passion, where He accomplished the glorious work of our redemption. They love to linger along that *Via Dolorosa* which leads from Gethsemane to Golgotha; let us linger with them.

When I stand and view my Lord, like the bush in Horeb, burning but not consumed, I hear a voice saying unto me, "The place whereon thou standest is holy ground." Nothing is more holy than the person of our divine Master; it is, therefore, well to be with Him. The anguish which He endured when He devoted His person as a sacrifice for us is holy too, and so it is well to be with Him in His sufferings. His sorrows have a most sanctifying influence upon all who consider them with believing love. I am persuaded that if we lived more in the atmosphere of the cross sin would lose its power, and every grace would flourish. When we draw very near

---

* This sermon is taken from *The Metropolitan Tabernacle Pulpit* and was preached on Sunday morning, February 12, 1882.

to Him and have fellowship with Him in His sufferings we raise a hue and cry against the sin which slew Him, and resolve to be revenged upon it by departing from it ourselves, and by warring against it whenever we see it in others. The cross is that holy implement with which we make war with sin till it be utterly destroyed. Blessed and holy, then, are the thoughts which are aroused by our great sacrifice.

Nor is it only so; but the medicine which brings us health is in itself a joy.

> Sweet the moments, rich in blessing,
> Which before the cross I spend,
> Life, and health, and peace possessing,
> In the sinner's dying Friend.

Here is no noise as of them that make merry over their wine, no shout of them that triumph, no song of them that feast; but here is a grave, sweet melody as of hearts that have found rest. At the cross we find a substantial joy, a far-reaching satisfaction, "the peace of God, which passeth all understanding." Here, restless ones, is the cure of restlessness: here shall you say, "O God, my heart is fixed, my heart is fixed. I will sing and give praise." I shall not, therefore, make any excuse, even if for weeks to come I should lead you to the place of dragons where your Lord was sore broken, and help you to drink of His cup, and to be baptized with His baptism. May the Spirit of God come upon and open our eyes to read the sacred heart of Him whose sorrows are unrivaled—sorrows born for love of us.

Let us go to the narrative at once with loving and lowly carefulness. Our Lord was condemned by the chief priests for blasphemy, because He declared Himself to be the Son of God, and told them that they should hereafter see Him coming in the clouds of heaven to be their judge. Rending His garments, the high priest said, "What need have we of any further witness? Ye have heard his blasphemy." When the morning light had come, and they had gone through the formality of a set trial by daylight, having really condemned Him in the night, they led Jesus away to Pilate. According to tradition, He was led with a rope about His neck, and His hands bound; and I can fully believe in the tradition when I remember the words of Isaiah: "He was led as a sheep to the slaughter." It was a strangely sad procession which moved through Jerusalem a little after six in the morning. Those men of the Sanhedrim in all their pomp and power surrounding this one poor victim, whom they were about to deliver to the Gentiles with the one design that he might be put to death! Those wicked men of pride were as the dogs of whom the Psalmist sang when the hind of the morning was His tender theme.

When they came to the house of the Roman governor, they would not themselves enter within its doors. It is said to have been one of the many magnificent palaces which Herod the Great built for himself; the architecture was gorgeous, the floors were inlaid with choice marbles, and all the chambers were richly gilded and furnished with Oriental splendor. Into the great hall these scrupulous hypocrites would not enter because they must by no means be defiled by the touch of a Gentile, for they had already commenced to keep the Passover. So they waited in the courtyard, and Pilate condescended to come out to them and learn the pressing business which brought them there so early in the morning. The Roman governor was proud, and cruel, and abhorred the Jews; but still, knowing their fanaticism and the readiness with which they broke loose at Passover times, he stood at his palace-gate and heard their demands. He soon ascertained that they had brought him a prisoner, evidently a poor man, and in personal appearance emaciated, weary, and suffering. About Him there was a mysterious dignity combined with singular gentleness, and Pilate for this and other reasons evidently took a singular interest in Him. Fixing his gaze first upon the extraordinary prisoner, he turned to the angry priests and demanded, "What accusation bring ye against this man?"

The one object of the priests in bringing Jesus to Pilate was to get Him put to death; for when Pilate told them to go and judge Him according to their law, they replied that they would gladly do so, but that the power of life and death had been taken from them, implying that nothing but His death would content them. They were, however, very anxious at this stage to lay the responsibility of His death upon the Romans, for the fear of the people was still upon them, and if they could secure His death by Pilate, then they might in after days protest that they merely handed Him over to the Roman governor and could not foresee that He would be handled so roughly. They had not yet bribed the populace to cry, "Crucify him," and they were willing to be on the safe side should the people make an uproar on His behalf. Humanly speaking, they could have put Him to death themselves, for He was entirely in their power, and they frequently forgot the Roman law and slew men in riotous fury, as when they stoned Stephen. They had frequently attempted to stone our Lord himself, so that they were not always to mindful of Roman law. They might have taken His life on this occasion, but they were led by a mysterious impulse to desire that the actual responsibility of the deed should rest on Pilate. Further on they were willing to join with the fickle throng in sharing the guilt of His blood, but as yet they would fain throw it upon others. During their great festivals if they took innocent blood, their hypocrisy made them wish to do it by forms of law and by an alien hand. To do this they must bring an accusation, for no Roman ruler would condemn a man till an accusation had been made.

We shall, this morning, consider *the two accusations* that they brought, and after that we shall hear *the verdict of acquittal* which Pilate gave in the language of the text: "I find in him no fault at all."

A Malefactor

The first accusation, if you will turn to the chapter and read verse 30, was that He was A MALEFACTOR. "They answered and said unto him, If he were not a malefactor, we would not have delivered him up unto thee." He was said to be a factor, or doer of that which is evil; a person of such a mischievous life that He ought not to live.

Upon which we remark, first, that *it was a novel charge*. It was hot from their mint; for when He stood before Caiaphas nothing was said of any evil that He had *done*, but only of evil that He had spoken. They charged Him with saying this and that, but not with doing any evil deed. The accusation of evil speaking had broken down, and they did not venture upon it a second time, because they knew very well that Pilate did not care what the man had said; all He would attend to would be some actual breach of law by act and deed. The Romans were a practical people, and so when Pilate led our Lord into the audience chamber he said to Him, "What has thou *done?*" He did not say to Him, "What hast thou taught or preached?" but, "What hast thou done?" For this reason, the priests brought forward this newly-invented accusation and totally unfounded charge that He was a bad doer, which might mean little or much, as the hearer chose to interpret it— malice is seldom specific in its charges. The accusation of being a malefactor grew out of their malevolence, and not out of any action of our Lord's perfect life. One is surprised that even hate should be so blind as to assail His perfections. Whatever men may think of our Lord as a teacher, candor demands that they admire His example and award it the highest meed of honor.

Observe, the priests herein brought against our Lord *a charge which they did not attempt to sustain*. How craftily they evaded the task of supplying proof! They brought no witnesses, their suborned perjurers were left behind; they even forbore from specific charges, but the general statement that He was a malefactor was supported only by their reputation. "If he were not a malefactor, we would not have delivered him up unto thee," as much as to say, "You must take it for granted that He is guilty, or we would not say so. Here is our high priest: can it be supposed that such a gem of an individual would bring a false accusation? We also are the chief priests and the scribes, and teachers of Israel: can it be imagined that persons of our station and sanctity could by any possibility have brought an innocent person before you to be condemned!" This style of argument I have heard even in these days: we are expected to give up the faith because scientists condemn it, and they are such eminent persons that we ought to accept their dicta without further delay. I confess I am not prepared to accept their infallibility any more than that which hails from Rome. The Roman governor was not to be overridden by priests, neither are we to be led by the nose by pretendedly learned men. "If he were not a malefactor, we would not have delivered him up unto thee." Oh, the hypocrisy of this speech! They had tried to bring witnesses, and no witness had been found. They had suborned false witnesses, but these had so differed in their testimony that the whole thing broke down. They, therefore, go upon another tack, and put their own names at the back of the indictment, as if that were quite enough, and inquiry need go no further. I think I see the scornful glance of Pilate as he bade them judge Him themselves if that was their style of justice; as for him, he must hear an accusation or dismiss them to do their own pleasure if they dare. He knew that through envy they had brought Jesus unto him, and he loathed the hypocrites as he heard the wretched syllables sibilating from their sanctimonious lips.

They could not have sustained the charge, and so far they were wise in not attempting the impossible. They might be foolhardy enough to wrest His words, but they hesitated before the task of attacking His deeds. Before His awful holiness they were for the moment out of heart, and knew not what slander to invent. O Lord, we marvel that any men should find fault with You, for You are altogether lovely, and there is in You no spot for falsehood to light upon. But I want to call your attention to this remarkable fact, that although this charge of being a malefactor was a grievous one, a trumped up one, and unsustained by any evidence, yet *it was never denied by the Lord Jesus Christ*. It was useless to deny it before the priests. He had already challenged them to find fault with His life, saying, "I spake openly to the world; I ever taught in the synagogue, and in the temple, whither the Jews always resort; and in secret have I said nothing. Why askest thou me? ask them which heard me, what I have said unto them: behold, they know what I said." His appeal had been unavailing, for it was as useless to argue with them as for a lamb to enter into controversy with a pack of wolves eager to devour. But there might have been some use, one would think, in His answering to Pilate, for Pilate was evidently very favorably impressed with his prisoner; and if the Savior had deigned to give a full account of His life, and to prove that instead of being a malefactor He had gone about doing good, might He not have escaped? The answer is this: our Lord had come on earth on purpose to be the substitute for guilty men, and so when He was called a malefactor, although it was not a truthful charge, yet He patiently bore the shame of it, as it is written, "He was numbered with the transgressors." He was willing to stand in the transgressor's place, and when they put Him there He did not stir from it. "He is dumb; he openeth not his mouth." He says nothing because, though in Him is no sin, He has taken our sin upon Himself. The question that Pilate put, "What hast thou done?" was one which Jesus might have grandly answered— "What have I done? I have fed the hungry, I have healed the sick, I have raised the fallen, I have restored the dead. What have I done? I have lived a self-sacrificing life, caring nothing for Myself or My own honor. I have been the vindicator of God and the friend of man. What have I done? Certainly nothing wherefore they could put Me to death, but everything why they should accept Me as their Leader and their Savior." We hear not a word of this. The exculpation would have been complete, but it was not spoken. He might have baffled His enemies as He had aforetime vanquished those who came to take Him, so that they went back to their masters, saying, "Never man spake like this man." He might have cleared Himself before the Roman procurator and by coming forth in triumph, He might have escaped from their teeth; but because He would stand in our stead, therefore when men imagined mischievous things against Him He was as a deaf man, and as a dumb man He opened not His mouth. Let us adore and bless Him for His gracious condescension, His matchless grace in standing in our stead.

Yet further, our Lord willed that by being counted as a transgressor by Pilate He might die the death appointed for malefactors by the Roman law. If the Jews had put our Lord to death for blasphemy, it would have been by stoning; but then, none of the prophecies that went before concerning the Messiah spoke of His being dashed to the ground by stones. The death ordained for Him was crucifixion. John says in the eighteenth chapter at the thirty-second verse, "That the saying of Jesus might be fulfilled, which he spake, signifying what death he should die." What was that saying? Is it not the saying in the twelfth chapter of John's gospel at the thirty-second verse, "I, if I be lifted up from the earth, will draw all men unto me. This he said, signifying what death he should die." Being lifted up from the earth on the cross was a death which could only come from the Romans; the Jews, as I have said before, executed men by stoning: therefore He must be condemned by the Romans that His own words may be fulfilled. He had spoken even more expressly in a passage recorded by Matthew, in the twentieth chapter at the seventeenth verse, where He had declared how He should die. "And Jesus going up to Jerusalem took the twelve disciples apart in the way, and said unto them, Behold, we go up to Jerusalem: and the Son of man shall be betrayed unto the chief priests and unto the scribes, and they shall condemn him to death, and shall deliver him to the Gentiles to mock, and to scourge, and to crucify him: and the third day he shall rise again." In order that the word which He had spoken might be fulfilled, our blessed master refused to plead before Pilate anything in answer to the question, "What hast thou done?" He stands as a transgressor, to die a transgressor's death; wherefore forever blessed be His adorable name for His voluntary endurance of penalty for our sakes.

When I think of that word "malefactor," another word leaps to my lips directly. Call Him not malefactor, but BENEFACTOR. What a benefactor must He be who in order to benefit us allows Himself to be branded as "malefactor"! Only think that He who at this moment sits in the center of adoring angels should have been called "malefactor"; that He from whose inexhaustible store of goodness all the saints in heaven and on earth are fed should yet be called "malefactor"; that He who never thought of harm of men, but whose very soul is love, whose every word and thought has been kindness toward this fallen race, should yet be called "malefactor." O earth, how could you bear so grave a lie against the infinite goodness of the Son of God! And yet, forever blessed be His name, He does not hurl back the charge, for that would have been to ruin us. He meekly bears the scandal for our sakes.

Should not this sweeten every title of reproach that can ever fall upon us? What if they call us ill names! They called the Master of the home "malefactor," can they call us anything worse? Shall we look for honor where our Captain found nothing but shame? Wherefore let it be our glory to bear shame and reproach for Jesus' sake. So much for the first accusation.

A King

Secondly, when the priests and scribes found that merely calling Him a malefactor was not sufficient, these wretched men changed their tactics, and, according to Luke, they charged Him with setting up to be A KING. They said that He wrought sedition, that He forbade to pay tribute unto Caesar, and made Himself out to be a king. These were three great lies, for Jesus had preached peace, and not sedition; His example was submission, not rebellion; His spirit was that of a servant, not that of a turbulent party leader. He had never said that men were not to pay tribute to Caesar; on the contrary, He had said, "Render unto Caesar the things that are Caesar's," and submitted Himself to every ordinance of authority. He had never in their sense set Himself up to be a king; if He had done so, many who were not His accusers might have been His partisans. The charge against Jesus of setting up to be a king in the sense in which they desired Pilate to understand them *was utterly false*, for when the multitude had been fed, they would have taken Him and made Him a king, but He hid Himself. Nay, so far from wishing to be a king, when one said to Him, "Master, speak to my brother that he divide the inheritance with me," He said, "Who made me a judge or a divider over you." He put aside any approach to interference with the reigning powers. His accusers must have known that if He had willed He had power at His back to have supported His claims, even as He said to Pilate, that, if He had been a king of a worldly dominion, His servants would have fought for Him. His followers had been brave and courageous, and enthusiastic, and they would, no doubt, have given no end of trouble both to the Jews and to the Romans if their leader had claimed a temporal sovereignty. But our Lord had made Peter put up his sword into its sheath. and healed the wound which he had given. All His life long He had preached peace and love, and a kingdom which is righteousness and peace. He was no rival to Caesar, and they knew it.

And please to notice that this charge of Christ being a king *did not come from the governing power.* When Pilate asked our Lord, "Art thou the King of the Jews?" our Savior wisely replied, "Sayest thou this of thyself, or did another tell thee it of me? Have you any reason to think that I am a leader of sedition? As the governor of this nation you have to watch carefully, for the people are seditious; have you ever seen or heard anything of me that looks like an attack on your authority? Have you anything of your own knowledge that would lead you to bring a charge against me?" Pilate, knowing nothing whatever against Him, and indeed scorning the idea that he knew anything about the Jewish people, whom he detested, replied haughtily, "Am I a Jew? Your own nation and your own rulers have brought this charge against you, not I." A great point was gained when Pilate said this; the charge was shown to be a mere invention, since the eagle eye of the Roman procurator had never seen the slightest ground for it.

It was a frivolous charge on the very face of it. How could that harmless, forsaken man be a peril to Caesar? What had the Roman legions to fear from that solitary sufferer? He was too meek and pure to threaten warfare and strife in the domain of Tiberius. Look at Him, and realize the absurdity of the situation. Moreover, it would seem a strange thing that the Jewish people should bring before the Roman governor their own king. Is this the way that subjects treat their monarchs? If He be a leader of sedition He does not seem to have succeeded with His countrymen, for the heads of the people are seeking His death. There could be upon the face of it no chance of danger whatever from rebellion which was so summarily put down by the Jews themselves. If they had not been besotted by their rage, they would themselves have shrunk from so absurd a position.

But yet I want you to note very carefully that *the Lord never denied this charge* in the sense in which He chose to understand it. He first explained what He meant by His being a king, and when He had explained it then He openly confessed that it was even so.

First, I say, *he explained what He meant by being a king*, and notice carefully that He did not explain it away. He said, "My kingdom," and also when Pilate said, "Art thou a king then?" He said, "Thou sayest that I am a king." He was there and then a real king, and He avowed it without reserve. We are constantly told that the kingdom of Christ is a spiritual kingdom, and this saying is true; but I would have you take heed that you do not spirit away His kingdom as if it were only a pious dream. Spiritual or not, the kingdom of Christ on earth is real and powerful. It is real nonetheless, but all the more, because it may fitly be called spiritual. Jesus is even now a king. He said, "I am a king." Some say that His kingdom is not yet, but is reserved for the latter days; but I aver that He is a king today, and that even now Jehovah has set Him as king upon the holy hill of Zion. I bless God that He has translated us "Into the kingdom of his dear Son."

"Thou art the king of glory, O Christ." When I say, "Thy kingdom come," I do not mean that it may begin to be set up on earth, but that it may continue to be set up in new places, may be extended and grow, for Jesus has at this very moment a kingdom upon the face of the earth, and they that know the truth belong to it, and recognize Him as the royal witness by whom the kingdom of truth has been founded and maintained. You remember the remarkable saying which is attributed to Napoleon Buonaparte in his later days at St. Helena: "I have founded a kingdom by force, and it has passed away; but Jesus founded His empire upon love, and therefore it will last forever." Verily, Napoleon spoke the truth—Jesus, the right royal Jesus, is Master of innumerable hearts today. The world knows Him not, but yet He has a kingdom in it which shall ere long break in pieces all other kingdoms. True and loyal hearts are to be found among the sons of men, and in them His name still wakes enthusiasm, so that for Him they are prepared to live and die. Our Lord is every inch a king, He has His throne of grace, has His scepter of truth, His officers who, like Himself, witness to the truth, and His armies of warriors who wrestle not with flesh and blood, and use no carnal weapons, but yet go forth conquering and to conquer. Our Lord has His palace wherein He dwells, His chariot in which He rides, His revenues, though they be not treasures of gold and silver, and His proclamations, which are law in His church. His reigning power affects the destiny of the world at this present moment far more than the counsels of the five great powers: by the preaching of the truth His servants shape the ages, and set up and cast down the thrones of earth. There is no prince so powerful as Jesus, and no empire so mighty as the kingdom of heaven.

Our Lord also said that His kingdom came not from this world; for that, I take it, is the more correct translation of the passage: "My kingdom is not of this world." It came not from this world; it is a substantial kingdom, but it did not spring from the same sources as the kingdoms of the world, neither is it supported, maintained, or increased by the same power as that which the kingdoms of the world depend upon. Christ's kingdom does not depend upon the force of arms: He would have His followers lay these weapons all aside. Christ's kingdom does not depend, as earthly kingdoms too often do, upon craft, policy, and duplicity. It used to be said that an ambassador was a gentleman who was sent abroad to lie for the good of his country, and I fear it might still describe full many an ambassador. What is the science of diplomacy but the art of deceit? When statesmen are thoroughly honest and are guided by principle, they are generally suspected, and an outcry is raised that the interests of the country will be sacrificed. But there is no diplomacy in Christ's rule; everything like crooked policy is of the devil, and not of Christ. He comes to bear witness to the truth, and it is by the truth, not by force nor by craft, that His throne is established among the sons of men, and therefore it is not from this world.

To be a king is indeed so little wrong in the sight of Jesus that it is the ultimate purpose of His coming to earth. He came to save men, did He not? Yes, but still He says, "For this purpose was I born, and for this cause came I into the world that I should bear witness unto the truth"; which is another way of saying, "that I might be a king." This is His ultimatum. Christ is a teacher that He may be a king; Christ is an example that He may be a king; Christ is a Savior that He may be a king; this is the great end and object that He has in His life, His death, His resurrection, and His second coming—that He may set up a kingdom among the sons of men to the glory of God. Oh that this great object of His mission might be furthered in our time, and consummated speedily in the long-promised age of gold.

The Master tells us that the main force and power of His kingdom lies in the truth. He came to be a King, but where is His scepter? The truth. Where is His sword? It comes out of His mouth: He bears witness to the truth. Where are His soldiers? They are men of truth. Jesus Christ leads on a band of whom He says, "And ye are my witnesses." His kingdom consists in witnessing to the truth, and who are they that become His subjects? Why, those that are of the truth, men who, hearing the truth, know the joyful sound and accept it, and feel its power.

Dear hearers, let each one of us ask himself, "Do I belong to His kingdom? Will I have this Man to reign over me? Do I desire to get rid of everything in myself that is not true? Am I anxious to put down around me everything that is false and wicked? Do I wish to uphold God's laws, for they are truth? Do I desire to spread the principles of love and kindness, for they are truth? Am I willing to learn, and so become the disciple of the greatest of all teachers, and, then, am I willing to bear witness to what I have learned, and so spread the sway of truth? If so, then I am of His kingdom. I know that I address many who desire in their hearts today that Christ and His truth may triumph, and they little mind what becomes of themselves. Let but His gospel spread and the principles of righteousness prevail; and as for us, let us live or die, it shall be a matter of small concern. O King, live forever, and we shall find our life in Your life, and glory in promoting Your glory, world without end. Such a spirit is of the truth, and we may assure ourselves that Jesus is our King.

Our Lord having explained His meaning, confessed that He was a King. This is that to which Paul refers when he says, "The Lord Jesus, who before Pontius Pilate witnessed a good confession." He did not draw back and say, "I am no King." Pilate might have delivered Him then; but He spoke boldly concerning His blessed, mysterious, and wonderful kingdom, and therefore it was not possible that He should be set free. This, indeed, was His accusation written over His cross, "This is Jesus the King of the Jews."

Poor Pilate, he did not understand our Lord, even as the men of this world understand not the kingdom of Christ. He said to Him, "What is truth?" and without waiting for a reply he went out to the Jews. Ah, brethren, let us never ourselves deny that Jesus is a king; but we shall deny it if we do not live according to His bidding. Oh you that claim to be Christ's, but do not live according to Christ's laws, you practically deny that He is a king. I dread the men who say, "We believe, and therefore we are saved," and then do not live in holiness; for these divide our Lord's offices, setting up His priesthood and denying His kingship. Half a Christ is no Christ—a Christ who is a priest but never a king is not the Christ of God. Oh brethren, live as those who feel that every word of Jesus is law, and that you must do what He bids you, as He bids you, and because He bids you; and so let all men know that unto you Jesus is both Lord and God.

The Acquittal

I conclude by noticing THE ACQUITTAL which Pilate gave to our Lord Jesus. He had heard the charge of being a malefactor, to which the prisoner pleaded nothing; He had heard the charge of His being a king, which the prisoner had most satisfactorily explained; and now Pilate coming out to the people said, "I find in him no fault at all." Pilate, you have spoken well. Your verdict is typical of the verdict of all who have ever *examined* Christ. Some have examined Him with an unfriendly eye, but in proportion as they have been candid in the observation of facts, they have been struck with His life and spirit. It is a very rare thing to hear even the infidel rail at the character of Jesus; in fact, some of the foremost skeptics as to our Lord's teaching have been remarkably impressed with admiration of His life. No character like that of Jesus is to be seen in history, nay not even in romance. If anyone says the four gospels are forgeries, let him try to write a fifth, which shall be like the other four. Why, you cannot add an incident to the life of Christ; its details are unique; the fancy cannot imagine a fresh incident which could be safely joined on to that which recorded. Every critic would cry out, "This is not genuine." The life of Jesus is a roll of cloth of gold, of the manufacture of which the art is utterly lost. His spotless character stands alone and by itself, and all true critics are compelled to say they find no fault at all in Him.

Let me add that this verdict of Pilate is the verdict of all that have ever *associated* with Christ. One disciple who was with Christ betrayed Him, but He spoke nothing against Him. Nay, the last witness of Judas before he hanged himself was this, "I have sinned in that I have betrayed the innocent blood." If there had been a fault in Jesus, the traitor would have spied it out; his unquiet conscience would have been glad enough to find therein a sedative, but even he was compelled to say, "I have betrayed the innocent blood." "Which of you convinceth me of sin?" is the challenge of Jesus, to which there is no reply.

Some of us have *lived with Christ spiritually.* In the course of His providence He has brought some of us very low by sickness, or by bereavement, or loss. Everyone saved by our Lord has come under the discipline of His house, for "whom the Lord loveth he chasteneth, and scrougeth every son whom he receiveth." Now, what is the verdict of all here present who know Jesus, our king? For my part, I find no fault at all in Him. He is everything that is lovely. He is all my salvation and all my desire. Do you not think that out of the millions of Christians who have lived hoping in Christ someone would have told us if it is His habit to disappoint His people? Out of so many believers who dwell with Him surely some one or other of them, when they came to die, would have told us if He is not all that He professes to be. Would not some one or other have confessed, "I trusted in Christ and He has not delivered me; it is all a delusion"? Surely, out of the many we have seen depart we should have found some one or two that would have let out the secret, and have said, "He is a deceiver. He cannot save, He cannot help, He cannot deliver." But never one dying believer throughout the ages has spoken ill of Him; but all have said, "We find no fault at all in Him."

Mark you, that will be the verdict of everyone among you all. If any of you reject Christ, when you shall stand at His judgment seat to be condemned because you believe not on Him, and when that withering word, "Depart, ye cursed!" shall consign you to your everlasting portion, you shall then be obliged to say, "I find no fault at all *in Him.*" There was no failure in His blood—the failure was in my want of faith; no failure in His Spirit—the failure was in my obstinate will; no failure in His promise— the failure was that I would not receive Him; there was no fault at all in Him. He never spurned me. He never refused to hear my prayers. If my Sundays were wasted, it was no fault of His; if I defied the gospel, it was no fault of His; if I have perished, my blood is at my own door. "I find no fault at all in Him." From all parts of creation shall go up one general attestation to His perfection. Heaven and earth and hell shall all join the common verdict, "We find no fault at all in Him."

I will send you away when I give you three practical words to think of. The first is this: Beware of an external religion, for the men that called Jesus malefactor and falsely accused Him were very religious people, and would not go into Pilate's hall for fear of polluting themselves. They were strong in rituals, but weak in morals. None are so inveterate against the principles of the gospel as those whose religion consists in form and ceremony but does not affect their hearts. I charge you and your hearts and not your garments. Follow Christ spiritually; follow Christ in your very souls, or else sacraments will be your ruin, and even in trying to keep yourselves from ceremonial defilement you will be defiling yourselves with hypocrisy.

The next thing is to charge you, dear friends, and to charge myself also, to shun all proud worldliness like that of Pilate. Pilate treats the whole matter cavalierly; he is a proud and haughty Roman; he hates the people whom he governs, and though he has a conscience, and at the first he shows a tenderness toward his prisoner, yet his chief end and aim was to keep his office and amass money, and therefore innocent blood must be spilt. He must please the Jews, even if he murder the "Just One." This selfish worldliness in which a man makes his gold and himself his god always treats religion with contempt. The man minds the main chance, and sneeringly cries, "What is truth?" He knows what money is and what power is, but what is truth? It is a dream, a folly to him, and he despises it. There are persons around us now, clever time-serving men, with grand notions of their own abilities, and to them Jesus and His gospel are matters for old women, servant girls, and what they call a Puritan crew. Such topics are not for gentlemen of thought, culture, and understanding, like their high and mighty selves. "What is truth?" say they. They are rather favorably inclined to religion, that is to say, they do not persecute, but they despise, which in some respects is worse. They say, "We are agnostics; we have no particular views; we are large-hearted, and let every man think as he chooses, but still there is nothing in it; it is all matter of opinion. One man says this is the truth, and another says that is the truth, and how are we to know? The fact is, there is no such thing as fixed truth at all.

> For differing creeds let graceless zealots fight;
> He can't be wrong whose life is in the right.

This is this great man's conclusion of the matter, and yet it so happens that this gentleman's life is not in the right at all, and therefore on his own showing he has not much joy of his pretty rhyme. I think I see him as he turns on His heel with, "What is truth?" Let him be a warning to you. Come not near to such arrogant trifling. Be always foolish enough to be willing to judge candidly. Be so little clever as to be willing still to learn. Be so little certain of your own infallibility that you will at least hear reason, and will inquire whether these things be so. Alas, I fear that through worldly pride many will have it said of them, as it is said of the Roman governor every day in the creed: "Suffered under Pontius Pilate." Oh, how many times has Christ suffered under just such people as Pontius Pilate

Last of all, let us all submit ourselves to Jesus our King. Wayworn and weary, emaciated and broken down, with his face more marred than that of any man, yet let us bow before Him and say, "All hail, thou King of the Jews. Thou art our King forever and ever." If we are willing thus to acknowledge Him as our King in His shame and derision, He will by-and-by honor us when He comes in the glory of the Father, and all His holy angels with Him. Then shall He cause it to be seen that He has made us who follow Him to be kings and priests unto God and we shall reign with Him forever and ever. Amen.

10

Barabbas Preferred to Jesus*

Then cried they all again, saying, Not this man, but Barabbas. Now Barabbas was a robber (John 18:40).

The custom of delivering a prisoner upon the day of the Passover was intended no doubt as an act of grace on the part of the Roman authorities toward the Jews, and by the Jews it may have been accepted as a significant compliment to their Passover. Since on that day they themselves were delivered out of the land of Egypt, they may have thought it to be most fitting that some imprisoned person should obtain his liberty. There was no warrant however in Scripture for this, it was never commanded by God, and it must have had a very injurious effect upon public justice, that the ruling authority should discharge a criminal, someone quite irrespective of his crimes or of his repentance; letting him loose upon society, simply and only because a certain day must be celebrated in a peculiar manner. Since some one prisoner must be delivered on the paschal day, Pilate thinks that he has now an opportunity of allowing the Savior to escape without at all compromising his character with the authorities at home. He asks the people which of the two they will prefer, a notorious thief then in custody, or the Savior. It is probable that Barabbas had been, up till that moment, obnoxious to the crowd; and yet, notwithstanding his former unpopularity—the multitude, instigated by the priests, forget all his faults, and prefer him to the Savior. Who Barabbas was, we cannot exactly tell. His name, as you in a moment will understand, even if you have not the slightest acquaintance with Hebrew, signifies "his father's son," "*Bar*" signifying "son," as when Peter is called Simon Bar-jonas, son of Jonas; the other part of his name "*Abbas*," signifying "father"—"abbas" being the word which we use in our filial aspirations, "Abba Father." Barabbas, then, is the "son of his father"; and some mys-

---

* This sermon is taken from *The Metropolitan Tabernacle Pulpit* and was preached on Sunday morning, October 16, 1864.

ticists think that there is an imputation here, that he was particularly and specially a son of Satan. Others conjecture that it was an endearing name, and was given him because he was his father's darling, an indulged child; his father's boy, as we say; and these writers add that indulged children often turn out to be imitators of Barabbas, and are the most likely persons to become injurious to their country, griefs to their parents, and curses to all about them. If it be so, taken in connection with the case of Absalom and especially of Eli's sons, it is a warning to parents that they err not in excessive indulgence of their children. Barabbas appears to have committed three crimes at the least: he was imprisoned for murder, for sedition, and for felony—a sorry combination of offenses, certainly; we may well pity the sire of such a son. This wretch is brought out and set in competition with Christ. The multitude are appealed to. Pilate thinks that from the sense of shame they really cannot possibly prefer Barabbas; but they are so bloodthirsty against the Savior, and are so moved by the priests, that with one consent—there does not appear to have been a single objecting voice, nor one hand held up to the contrary—with a marvelous unanimity of vice, they cry, "Not this man, but Barabbas," though they must have known, since he was a *notable* well-known offender, that Barabbas was a murderer, a felon, and a traitor.

This fact is very significant. There is more teaching in it than at first sight we might imagine. Have we not here, first of all, in this act of the deliverance of the sinner and the binding of the innocent, a sort of type of that great work which is accomplished by the death of our Savior? You and I may fairly take our stand by the side of Barabbas. We have robbed God of His glory; we have been seditious traitors against the government of heaven: if he who hates his brother be a murderer, we also have been guilty of that sin. Here we stand before the judgment seat; the Prince of Life is bound for us and we are suffered to go free. The Lord delivers us and acquits us, while the Savior, without spot or blemish, or shadow of a fault, is led forth to crucifixion. Two birds were taken in the rite of the cleansing of a leper. The one bird was killed, and its blood was poured into a basin; the other bird was dipped in this blood, and then, with its wings all crimson, it was set free to fly into the open field. The bird slain well pictures the Savior, and every soul that has by faith been dipped in His blood, flies upward toward heaven singing sweetly in joyous liberty, owing its life and its liberty entirely to Him who was slain. It comes to this, Barabbas must die or Christ must die; you the sinner must perish, or Christ Immanuel, the Immaculate, must die. He dies that we may be delivered. Oh! have we all a participation in such a deliverance today? And though we have been robbers, traitors, and murderers yet we can rejoice that Christ has delivered us from the curse of the law, having been made a curse for us?

The transaction has yet another voice. This episode in the Savior's history shows that in the judgment of the people, Jesus Christ was a greater offender than Barabbas; and, for once, I may venture to say, that *vox populi* (the voice of the people), which in itself was a most infamous injustice, if it be read in the light of the imputation of our sins to Christ, was *vox Dei* (the voice of God). Christ, as He stood covered with His people's sins, had more sin laid upon Him than that which rested upon Barabbas. In Him was no sin; He was altogether incapable of becoming a sinner: holy, harmless, and undefiled is Christ Jesus, but He takes the whole load of His people's guilt upon Himself by imputation, and as Jehovah looks upon Him, He sees more guilt lying upon the Savior, than even upon this atrocious sinner, Barabbas. Barabbas goes free—innocent—in comparison with the tremendous weight which rests upon the Savior. Think, beloved, then, how low your Lord and Master stooped to be thus *numbered with the transgressors*. Watts has put it strongly, but, I think, none too strongly—

> His honor and his breath
> Were taken both away,
> Join'd with the wicked in his death,
> And made as vile as they.

He was so in the estimation of the people, and before the bar of justice, for the sins of the whole company of the faithful were made to meet upon Him. "The Lord hath laid upon him the iniquity of us all." What that iniquity must have been, no heart can conceive, much less can any tongue tell. Measure it by the griefs He bore, and then, if you can guess what these were, you can form some idea of what must have been the guilt which sunk Him lower before the bar of justice than even Barabbas himself. Oh! what condescension is here! The just One dies for the unjust. He bears the sin of many, and makes intercession for the transgressors.

Yet, again, there seems to me to be a third lesson, before I come to that which I want to enforce from the text. Our Savior knew that His disciples would in all ages be hated by the world far more than outward sinners. Full often the world has been more willing to put up with murderers, thieves, and drunkards, than with Christians; and it has fallen to the lot of some of the best and most holy of men to be so slandered and abused that their names have been cast out as evil, scarcely worthy to be written in the same list with criminals. Now, Christ has sanctified these sufferings of His people from the slander of their enemies, by bearing just such sufferings Himself so that, my brethren, if you or I should find ourselves charged with crimes which we abhor, if our heart should be ready to burst under the accumulation of slanderous venom, let us lift up our head and feel that in all this we have a comrade who has true fellowship with us, even the Lord Jesus Christ, who was rejected when Barabbas was selected. Expect no better treatment than your Master. Remember that the disciple is not above his Lord. If they have called the Master of the house Beelzebub, much more will they call them of His household; and if they prefer the murderer to Christ, the day may not be distant when they will prefer even a murderer to you.

These things seem to me to lie upon the surface; I now come to our more immediate subject. First, we shall consider *the sin as it stands in the Evangelical history*; secondly, we shall observe that *this is the sin of the whole world*; thirdly, that *this sin we ourselves were guilty of before conversion*; and fourthly, that *this is, we fear, the sin of very many persons who are here this morning*: we shall talk with them and expostulate, praying that the Spirit of God may change their hearts and lead them to accept the Savior.

The Sin as It Stands in the Evangelical History

A few minutes may be profitably spent in CONSIDERING, THEN, THE SIN AS WE FIND IT IN THIS HISTORY.

They preferred Barabbas to Christ. The sin will be more clearly seen if we remember that *the Savior had done no ill*. No law, either of God or man, had He broken. He might truly have used the cords of Samuel— "behold, here I am: witness against me before the Lord, and before his anointed: whose ox have I taken? or whose ass have I taken? or whom have I defrauded? whom have I oppressed? or of whose hand have I received any bribe to blind mine eyes therewith? and I will restore it you." Out of that whole assembled crowd there was not one who would have had the presumption to accuse the Savior of having done him damage. So far from this, they could but, acknowledge that *He had even conferred great temporal blessings upon them*. O ravening multitude, has He not fed you when you were hungry? Did He not multiply the loaves and fishes for you? Did He not heal your lepers with His touch? Cast out devils from your sons and daughters? Raise up your paralytics? Give sight to your blind, and open the ears of your deaf? For which of these good works do you conspire to kill Him? Among that assembled multitude, there were doubtless some who owed to Him priceless boons, and yet, though all of them his debtors if they had known it, they clamor against Him as though He were the worst trouble of their lives, a pest and a pestilence to the place where He dwelt.

Was it His teaching that they complained of? Wherein did His teaching offend against morality? Wherein against the best interests of man? If you observe the teaching of Christ there was never any like it, even judged of by how far it would subserve human welfare. Here was the sum and substance of His doctrine, "Thou shalt love the Lord thy God with all thy heart, and thy neighbor as thyself." His precepts were of the mildest form. Did He bid them draw the sword and expel the Roman, or ride on in a ruthless career of carnage and rapine? Did He stimulate them to let loose their unbridled passions? Did He tell them to seek first of all their own advantage and not to care for their neighbor's weal? Nay, every righteous state must own Him to be its best pillar, and the commonwealth of manhood must acknowledge Him to be its conservator; and yet, for all this, there they are, hounded on by their priests, seeking His blood, and crying, "Let him be crucified! let him be crucified!"

His whole intent evidently was their good. What did He preach for? No selfish motive could have been urged. Foxes had holes, and the birds of the air had nests, but He had not where to lay His head. The charity of a few of His disciples alone kept Him from absolute starvation. Cold mountains, and the midnight air, witnessed the fervor of His lonely prayers for the multitudes who now are hating Him. He lived for others: they could see this; they could not have observed Him during the three years of His ministry without saying, "Never lived there such an unselfish soul as this"; they must have known, the most of them, and the rest might have known, had they inquired ever so little, that He had no object whatever in being here on earth, except that of seeking the good of men. For which of these things do they clamor that He may be crucified? For which of His good works, for which of His generous words, for which of His holy deeds will they fasten His hands to the wood, and His feet to the tree? With unreasonable hatred, with senseless cruelty, they only answer to the question of Pilate, "Why, what evil hath he done?" "Let him be crucified! let him be crucified!"

The true reason of their hate, no doubt, lay in the natural hatred of all men to perfect goodness. Man feels that the presence of goodness is a silent witness against his own sin, and therefore he longs to get rid of it. To be too holy in the judgment of men is a great crime, for it rebukes their sin. If the holy man has not the power of words, yet his life is one loud witness-bearing for God against the sins of His creatures. This inconvenient protesting led the wicked to desire the death of the holy and just One. Besides, the priests were at their backs. It is a sad and lamentable thing, but it is often the case that the people are better than their religious teachers. At the present moment the laity of the Church of England, as a whole, have honest consciences, and would have their Prayer Book revised tomorrow if their voices could be heard. But their clerics care far too little about truth, and are not very particular how they swear, or with whom they associate. So long as their church can be kept together, Father Ignatius shall be heard in their assemblies, although Christ's call to the church to purify herself awakens only resentment and ill-will. No matter that the throats of certain clergymen were exercised in hissing for a moment at the apparition of the bold Anglican monk, he is one of themselves, a brother of their own order, and their church is responsible for all that he does. Let them come out and separate themselves, and then we shall know that they abhor this modern popery; but so long as they sit in the same assembly and are members of the same church, the sin is theirs, and we shall not cease to denounce both it and them. If Evangelical clergymen remain in communion with Papists, now that they come out in their full colors, I will cease to say that they violate their consciences, but I shall doubt whether they have any consciences at all. Brethren, it is still the case that the people are better than their teachers. This people would not have crucified Christ had not the clergy of the day, the priests, the endowed ministers, cried out, "Let him be crucified!" He was the dissenter, the heretic, schismatic, the troubler in Israel. He it was who cried aloud against the faults of their establishment. He it was who could not be put down, the *ignorant* man from Galilee, who would continue to clamor against them, the mischief-maker, and therefore "Let him be crucified! Let him be crucified!" Anything is good enough for the man who talks about reform, and advocates changes in established rules. No doubt bribery also was used in this case. Had not Rabbi Simon paid the multitude? Was there not a hope of some feast after the Passover was over to those who would use their throats against the Savior? Beside, there was the multitude going that way; and so if any had compassion they held their tongue. Often they say that "Discretion is the better part of valor"; and truly there must be many valorous men, for they have much of valor's better part, discretion. If they did not join in the shout, yet at least they would not incommode the others, and so there was but one cry, "Away with him! away with him! It is not fit that he should live." What concentrated scorn there is this fortieth verse. It is not "this Jesus," they would not foul their mouths with His name, but this *fellow*—"this devil," if you will. To Barabbas they give the respect of mentioning his name; but "this—" whom they hate so much, they will not even stoop to mention. We have looked, then, at this great sin as it stands in the history.

The Sin of the Whole World

But now let us look, in the second place, AT THIS INCIDENT AS SETTING FORTH THE SIN WHICH HAS BEEN THE GUILT OF THE WORLD IN ALL AGES, AND WHICH IS THE WORLD'S GUILT NOW.

When the apostles went forth to preach the gospel, and the truth had spread through many countries, there were severe edicts passed by the Roman Emperors. Against whom were these edicts framed? Against the foul offenders of that day? It is well known that the whole Roman Empire was infested with vices such as the cheek of modesty would blush to hear named. The first chapter of the Epistle to the Romans is a most graphic picture of the state of society throughout the entire Roman dominions. When severe laws were framed, why were they not proclaimed against these atrocious vices? It is scarcely fit that men should go unpunished who are guilty of crimes such as the apostle Paul has mentioned, but I find no edicts against these things—I find that they were born with and scarcely mentioned with censure; but burning, dragging at the heels of wild horses, the sword, imprisonment, tortures of every kind, were used against whom think you? Against the innocent, humble followers of Christ, who, so far from defending themselves, were willing to suffer all these things, and presented themselves like sheep at the shambles, willing to endure the butcher's knife. The cry of the world, under the persecutions of Imperial Rome, was "Not Christ, but Sodomites, and murderers, and thieves—we will bear with any of these, but not with Christ; away with His followers from the earth." Then the world changed its tactics; it became nominally Christian, and Antichrist came forth in all its blasphemous glory. The Pope of Rome put on the triple crown, and called himself the Vicar of Christ; then came in the abomination of the worship of saints, angels, images, and pictures; then came the mass, and I know not what, of detestable error; and what did the world say? "Popery forever!" Down went every knee, and every head bowed before the sovereign representative of Peter at Rome. The Church of Rome was equal in sin to Barabbas; nay, I do but compliment Barabbas when I mention him in the same breath with many of the popes, for their character was foul and black right through and through, till even those who superstitiously looked upon them as infallible in their office, could not defend their personal characters. The world chose the harlot of Rome, and she who was drunk with the wine of her abominations had every eye to gaze upon her with admiration, while Christ's gospel was forgotten, buried in a few old books, and almost extinguished in darkness. Since that day the world has changed its tactics yet again; in many parts of the earth Protestantism is openly acknowledged, and the gospel is preached, but what then? Then comes in Satan, and another Barabbas, the Barabbas of mere ceremonialism, and mere attendance at a place of worship is set up. "Yes, we are orthodox; so orthodox, so sound. Yes, we are religious, strictly religious; we attend our meeting house, or go to our church. We are never absent. We attend every form, but we have no vital godliness; we have not been born again; we have not passed from death unto life." However, this will do; so long as we are as good as our neighbors, and keep the outward rite, the inward does not matter. This which is a foul robbery of God's glory, this which murders men's souls, is the Barabbas of the present age. An outward name to live is set up, and is received by those who are dead; and many of you now present are quite easy and content, though you have never felt the quickening Spirit of God: though you have never been washed in the atoning blood, yet you are satisfied because you take a seat in some place of worship; you give your guinea, your donation to a hospital, or your subscription to a good object, forgetting and not caring to remember that all the making clean of the outside of the cup and the platter will never avail, unless the inward nature be renewed by the Spirit of the living God. This is the great Barabbas of the present age, and men prefer it before the Savior.

That this is true, that the world really loves sin better than Christ, I think I could prove clearly enough by one simple fact. You have observed sometimes Christian men inconsistent, have you not? The inconsistency was nothing very great, if you had judged them according to ordinary rules of conduct. But you are well aware that a worldly man might commit any sin he liked, without much censure; but if the Christian man commits ever so little, then hands are held up, and the whole world cries, "Shame!" I do not want to have that altered, but I do want just to say this: "There is Mr. So-and-So, who is known to live a fast, wicked, carefree life; well, I do not see that he is universally avoided and reprobated, but on the contrary, he is tolerated by most, and admired by some." But suppose a Christian man, a well-known professor, to have committed some fault which, compared with this, were not worth mentioning, and what is done? "Oh! publish it! publish it! Have you heard what Mr. So-and-So did? Have you heard of this hypocrite's transgression?" "Well, what was it?" You look at it: "Well, it is wrong, it is very wrong, but compared with what you say about it is nothing at all." The world therefore shows by the difference between the way in which it judges the professedly religious man, and that with which it judges its own, that it really can tolerate the most abandoned, but cannot tolerate the Christian. Of course, the Christian never will be altogether free from imperfections; the world's enmity is not against the Christian's imperfections evidently, because they will tolerate greater imperfections in others; the objection must therefore be against the man, against the profession which he has taken up, and the course which he desires to follow. Watch carefully, beloved, that you give them no opportunity; but when you see that the slightest mistake is laid hold of and exaggerated, in this you see a clear evidence that the world prefers Barabbas to the followers of the Lord Jesus Christ. Now the world will change its various modes of dealing, but it will never love the church better than it does now. We do not expect to see the world lifted up to become more and more absorbed into the church. The union of the world with the church was never the object of our religion. The object of Christ is to gather to Himself a people from among men; it is not the lifting up of all, but the calling out of the some, the making of men to differ, the manifestation of His special and discriminating grace, the gathering together of a people whom He has formed for Himself. In this process morality is promoted, men are civilized and improved, but this is only indirectly God's object, and not His immediate end; the immediate end of the gospel being the salvation of the people whom He has ordained unto eternal life, and who, therefore, in due season are led to believe in Him. The world, to the end of the chapter, will be as much at enmity with true believers as ever it was. Because "ye are not of the world, therefore the world hateth you." This will be as true when Christ shall come as at the present moment. Let us expect it; and when we meet with scorn and persecution, let us not be surprised as though some strange thing had happened unto us.

The Sin We Ourselves Were Guilty of Before Conversion

I come in the third place, and O for some assistance from on high, to observe that THE SIN OF PREFERRING BARABBAS TO CHRIST WAS THE SIN OF EVERY ONE OF US BEFORE OUR CONVERSION.

Will you turn over the leaves of your diary, now, dear friends, or fly upon the wings of memory to the hole of the pit whence you were digged. Did you not, O you who live close to Christ, did you not once despise Him? What company did you like best? Was it not that of the frivolous, if not that of the profane? When you sat with God's people, their talk was very tedious; if they spoke of divine realities, and of experimental subjects, you did not understand them, you felt them to be troublesome. I can look back upon some whom I know now to be most venerable believers, whom I thought to be a gross nuisance when I heard them talk of the things of God. What were our thoughts about? When we had time for thinking, what were our favorite themes? Not much did we meditate upon eternity; not much upon Him who came to deliver us from the misery of hell's torments. Brethren, His great love wherewith He loved us was never laid to heart by us as it should have been; nay, if we read the story of the crucifixion, it had no more effect upon our mind than a common tale. We knew not the beauties of Christ; we thought of any trifle sooner than of Him. And what were our pleasures? When we had what we called a day's enjoyment, where did we seek it? At the foot of the cross? In the service of the Savior? In communion with Him? Far from it; the further we could remove from godly associations the better pleased we were. Some of us have to confess with shame that we were never more in our element than who we were without a conscience, when conscience ceased to accuse us and we could plunge into sin with riot. What was our reading then? Any book sooner than the Bible: and if there had lain in our way anything that would have exalted Christ and extolled Him in our understandings, we should have put by the book as much too dry to please us. Any three-volume heap of nonsense, any light literature; nay, perhaps, even worse would have delighted our eye and our heart; but thoughts of *His* eternal delight toward us—thoughts of His matchless passion and His glory now in heaven, never came across our minds, nor would we endure those who would have led us to such meditations. What were our aspirations then? We were looking after business, aiming at growing rich, famous for learning or admired for ability. Self was what we lived for. If we had some regard for others, and some desire to benefit our race, yet self was at the bottom of it all. We did not live for God—we could not honestly say, as we woke in the morning, "I hope to live for God today"; at night, we could not look back upon the day, and say, "We have this day served God." He was not in all our thoughts. Where did we spend our best praise? Did we praise Christ? No; we praised cleverness, and when it was is association with sin, we praised it none the less. We admired those who could most fully minister to our own fleshly delights, and felt the greatest love to those who did us the worst injury. Is not this our confession as we review the past? Have I not read the very history of your life? I know I have of my own. Alas! for those dark days, which our besotted soul went after any evil, but would not follow after Christ. It would have been the same today with us, if almighty grace had not made the difference. We may as well expect the river to cease to run to the sea, as expect the natural man to turn from the current of his sins. As well might we expect fire to become water, or water to become fire, as for the unrenewed heart ever to love Christ. It was mighty grace which made us to seek the Savior. And as we look back upon our past lives, it must be with mingled feelings of gratitude for the change, and of sorrow that we should have been so grossly foolish as to have chosen Barabbas, and have said of the Savior, "Let him be crucified!"

The Sin of Many Yet Today

And now I shall come to the closing part of the sermon, which is, THAT THERE ARE DOUBTLESS MANY HERE WHO THIS DAY PREFER BARABBAS TO OUR LORD JESUS CHRIST.

Let me first state your case, dear friends. I would describe it honestly, but at the same time so describe it that you will see your sin in it; and while I am doing so, my object will be to expostulate with you, if haply the Lord may change your will. There are many here, I fear, who prefer sin to Christ. I may say, without making a guess, I know that there are those here who would long ago have been followers of Christ, but that they preferred drunkenness. It is not often, it is not every day, it is not even every week, but there are occasions when they feel as if they must go into company, and as a sure result they return home intoxicated. They are ashamed of themselves—they have expressed as much as that; they have even gone so far as to pray to God for grace to overcome their habit; but after being the subject of convictions for years, they have hitherto made no advance. It did seem once as if they had conquered it. For a long time there was an abstinence from the fault, but they have gone back to their folly. They have preferred the bestial degrading vice—shall I say bestial? I insult the beasts, for they are not guilty of such a vice as this—they prefer this degrading vice to Christ Jesus. There stands drunkenness, I see it mirrored before me with all its folly, its witnesses, its greed and filth; but the man chooses all that, and though he has known by head knowledge something concerning the beauty and excellency of Christ, he virtually says of Jesus, "Not this man, but drunkenness."

Then there are other cases, where a favorite lust reigns supreme in their hearts. The men know the evil of the sin, and they have good cause to know it; they know also something of the sweetness of religion, for they are never happier than when they come up with God's people; and they go home sometimes from a solemn sermon, especially if it touches their vice, and they feel, "God has spoken to my soul today, and I am brought to a standstill." But for all that, the temptation comes again, and they fall as they have fallen before. I am afraid there are some of you whom no arguments will ever move; you have become so set on this mischief that it will be your eternal ruin. But oh! think you, how will this look when you are in hell— "I preferred that foul Barabbas of lust to the beauties and perfections of the Savior, who came into the world to seek and to save that which was lost!" and yet this is the case, not of some, but of a great multitude who listen to the gospel, and yet prefer sin to its saving power.

There may be some here, too, of another class, who prefer *gain*. It has come to this: if they become truly the Lord's people, they cannot do in trade what they now think their trade requires them to do; if they become really and genuinely believers, they must of course become honest, but their trade would not pay, they say, if it were conducted upon honest principles; or it is such a trade, and there are some such, as ought not to be conducted at all, much less by Christians. Here comes the turning point. Shall I take the gold, or shall I take Christ? True, it is cankered gold, and gold on which a curse must come. It is the fool's pence, may be it is gain that is extorted from the miseries of the poor; is money that would not ever stand the light because it is not fairly come by; money that will burn its way right through your souls when you get upon your deathbeds; but yet men who love the world, say, "No, not Christ, give me a full purse, and away with Christ." Others, less base or less honest, "We know His excellence, we wish we could have Him, but we cannot have Him on terms which involve the renunciation of our dearly-beloved gain." "Not this man, but Barabbas."

Others say, "I fain would be a Christian, but then I should lose many of my acquaintances and friends. For the matter of what it comes to, my friends are not much good to me; they are such friends as are fondest when I have most money to spend with them; they are friends who praise me most when I am most often at the ale-house, when I am seen plunging deepest into their vices. I know they do me mischief, but," says the man, "I could not venture to oppose them. One of them has such a glib tongue, and he can make such telling jokes, I could not bear to have him down upon me; and there is another. I have heard him give Christians such stinging names, and point their faults in such a sarcastic manner, I could not run the gauntlet of his tongue; and therefore, though I fain would be a Christian, yet I will not." That is the way you prefer to be a serf, a slave to the tongue of the scorner, sooner than be a free man, and take up the cross and follow Christ. You prefer, I say, not merely by way of allegory, but as matter of fact, you prefer Barabbas to the Lord Jesus Christ.

I might thus multiply instances, but the same principle runs through them all. If anything whatever keeps you back from giving your heart to the Lord Jesus Christ, you are guilty of setting up an opposition candidate to Christ in your soul, and you are choosing "not this man, but Barabbas." Let me occupy a few minutes with pleading Christ's cause with you. Why is it that you reject Christ? Are you not conscious of the many good things which you receive from Him? You would have been dead if it had not been for Him; nay, worse than that, you would have been in hell. God has sharpened the great ax; justice, like a stern woodsman, stood with the ax uplifted, ready to cut you down as a cumberer of the ground. A hand was seen stopping the arm of the avenger, and a voice was heard saying, "Let it alone, till I dig about it and dung it." Who was it that appeared just then in your moment of extremity? It was no other than that Christ, of whom you think so little that you prefer drunkenness or vice to Him! You are this day in the house of God, listening to a discourse which I hope is sent from Him. You might have been in hell—think one moment of that—shut out from hope, enduring in body and soul unutterable pangs. That you are not there should make you love and bless Him, who has said, "Deliver him from going down into the pit." Why will you prefer your own gain and self-indulgence to that blessed One to whom you owe so much. Common gratitude should make you deny yourself something for Him who denied Himself so much that He might bless you. Do I hear you say that you cannot follow Christ, because His precepts are too severe? In what respect are they too severe? If you yourself were set to judge them, what is the point with which you would find fault? They deny you your sins—say, they deny you your miseries. They do not permit you, in fact, to ruin yourself. There is no precept of Christ which is not for your good, and there is nothing which He forbids you which He does not forbid on the principle that it would harm you to indulge in it. But suppose Christ's precepts to be ever so stern, is it not better that you should put up with them than be ruined? The soldier submits implicitly to the captain's command, because he knows that without discipline there can be no victory, and the whole army may be cut in pieces if there be a want of order. When the sailor has risked his life to penetrate through the thick ice of the north, we find him consenting to all the orders and regulations of authority, and bearing all the hardships of the adventure, because he is prompted by the desire of assisting in a great discovery, or stimulated by large reward. And surely the little self-denials which Christ calls us to will be abundantly recompensed by the reward He offers; and when the soul and its eternal interests are at stake, we may well put up with these temporary inconveniences if we may inherit eternal life. I think I hear you say that you would be a Christian, but there is no happiness in it. I would not tell you a falsehood on this point, I would speak the truth if it were so, but I do solemnly declare that there is more joy in the Christian life than there is in any other form of life; that if I had to die like a dog, and there were no hereafter, I would prefer to be a Christian. You shall appeal to the very poorest among us, to those who are most sick and most despised, and they will tell you the same. There is not an old country woman shivering in her old ragged red cloak over a handful of fire, full of rheumatism, with an empty cupboard and an aged body, who would change with the very highest and greatest of you if she had to give up her religion; no, she would tell you that her Redeemer was a greater comfort to her than all the luxuries which could be heaped upon the table of Dives. You make a mistake when you dream that my Master does not make His disciples blessed; they are a blessed people who put their trust in Christ. Still I think I hear you say, "Yes, this is all very well, but still I prefer *present* pleasure." Do you not in this talk like a child; nay, like a fool, for what is present pleasure? How long does that word "present" last? If you could have ten thousand years of merriment I might agree with you in a measure, but even there I should have but short patience with you, for what would be ten thousand years of sin's merriment compared with millions upon millions of years of sin's penalty. Why, at the longest, your life will be but very short. Are you not conscious that time flies more hurriedly every day? As you grow older, do you not seem as if you had lived a shorter time instead of longer? Until, perhaps, if you could live to be as old as Jacob, you would say, "Few and evil have my days been," for they appear fewer as they grow more numerous. You know that this life is but a span, and is soon over. Look to the graveyards, see how they are crowded with green mounds. Remember your own companions, how one by one they have passed away. They were as firm and strong as you, but they have gone like a shadow that declines. Is it worthwhile to have this snatch space of pleasure, and then to lie down in eternal pain? I pray you to answer this question. Is it worthwhile to choose Barabbas for the sake of the temporary gain he may give you, and give up Christ, and so renounce the eternal treasures of joy and happiness which are at His right hand forevermore? I wish that I could put these questions before you as they ought to be put. It needs the earnest seraphic voice of Whitfield, or the pleading tongue of Richard Baxter, to plead with you, but yet I think I talk to rational men; and if it be a matter of arithmetic, it shall need no words of mine. I will not ask you to take your life at the longest that you expect it to be—at eighty, say—crowd it full of all the pleasures you can imagine; suppose yourself in good health; dream yourself to be without business cares, with all that heart can wish; go and sit upon the throne of Solomon if you will, yet what will you have to say when it is all over? Looking back upon it, can you make more of it than Solomon did, when he said, "Vanity of vanities, all is vanity"—"All is vanity and vexation of spirit"? When you have cast up that sum, may I ask you to calculate how much you will have gained, if, in order to possess this vanity, you have renounced eternal happiness, and have incurred everlasting woe? Do you believe the Bible? You say, "Yes." Well, then, it must so. Many men profess to be believers in Scripture, and yet, when you come to the point as to whether they do believe in eternal woe and eternal joy, there is a kind of something inside which whispers, "That is in the Book—but still it is not real, it is not true to us." Make it true to yourselves, and when you have so done it, and have clearly proved that you must be in happiness or woe, and that you must here either have Barabbas for your master, or have Christ for your Lord, then, I say, like sane men, judge which is the better choice, and may God's mighty grace give you spiritual sanity to make the right choice; but this I know, you never will unless that mighty Spirit who alone leads us to choose the right, and reject the wrong, shall come upon you and lead you to fly to a Savior's wounds.

I need not, I think, prolong the service now, but I hope you will prolong it at your own houses by thinking of the matter. And may I put the question personally to all as you separate, whose are you? On whose side are you? There are no neuters; there are no betweenites: you either serve Christ or Belial; you are either with the Lord or with His enemies. Who is on the Lord's side this day? Who? Who is for Christ and for His cross; for His blood, and for His throne? Who, on the other hand, are His foes? As many as are not for Christ are numbered with His enemies. Be not so numbered any longer, for the gospel comes to you with an inviting voice— "Believe in the Lord Jesus Christ, and thou shalt be saved." God help you to believe and cast yourself upon Him now; and if you trust Him, you are saved now, and you shall be saved forever. Amen.

11

Stephen's Martyrdom *

But he, being full of the Holy Spirit, looked up steadfastly into heaven, and saw the glory of God, and Jesus standing on the right hand of God, and said, Behold, I see the heavens opened, and the Son of Man standing on the right hand of God (Acts 7:55–56).

True Christian zeal will seek to do the highest work of which sanctified humanity is capable. Stephen is first heard of as a distributor of the alms of the church to needy widows. He exercised what was virtually, if not nominally, the deacon's office. Being grave, and not double-tongued, and holding the mystery of the faith in a good conscience, he was well fitted for his work. Doubtless he used the office of a deacon well, and so purchased to himself a good degree, and great boldness in the faith which is in Christ Jesus. Although the onerous duty of serving tables might well have excused him from other service, we soon find him, full of faith and power, doing wonders and miracles among the people; and not even content with that, we see him defending the faith against a synagogue of subtle philosophical deniers of the truth. These, with their allies, made the valiant deacon the object of their attack and he at once rose to be an irresistible witness for the gospel. Stephen the deacon became Stephen the preacher. This holy man not only used such gifts as he had in one department, but having abilities for a more spiritual form of service, he laid them at once upon the altar of Christ. Nor is this all, he had a higher promotion yet—when he had thus become Stephen the wise apologist and brave defender of the faith, he did not stop there, but he mounted the highest rank of the Christian army; he gained the peerless dignity, the foremost nobility, the brightest glory—I mean the martyr's name and honor. Stephen the deacon is first Stephen the preacher, and afterward Stephen God's faithful and true witness, laying down his life that he may seal his testimony

---

* This sermon is taken from *The Metropolitan Tabernacle Pulpit* and was preached on Sunday morning, March 17, 1867.

134

with his blood. Put a man without zeal into the front place, and he will gradually recede into his native insignificance, or only linger in the front to be a impediment and a nuisance; but put a man into the rear of the army of God's elect, if his soul be full of holy fire, you will soon hear of the unknown Samson in the camps of Dan, and, ere long, he will dash into the vanguard, and make the enemies of God's church know that the Holy Spirit still dwells in the midst of Zion in the men whom he has chosen. If there be any of my brethren and sisters here whose abilities are as yet dormant, I trust that, without ambitiously seeking the chief places of the synagogue, if they have been useful in any one walk of life, they will inquire whether they may not have talents for a yet wider sphere; since, in these evil days, we have need to use every soldier in "the army to the utmost of his capacity." When the world is so dark, we had need that every lamp should give some light, and that each lamp should burn as much oil as it will carry, that its light may be of the brightest possible kind.

Stephen, as a martyr, is set before us in the words of our text. I shall not so much look upon him as witnessing for the truth, as ask you to look, first, at *the power of the Holy Spirit in him that you may learn to rely upon that divine power;* secondly, I shall *ask you to look at the source of his dying comfort that you may learn to gaze upon the same ravishing vision;* and, thirdly, I shall *bid you notice the effect of this heavenly comfort upon him, in the hope that we may live in peace and fall asleep in ease, by faith in the same great sight which cheered his dying eyes.*

The Power of the Holy Spirit as Developed in Stephen's Death

First, then, this morning, I shall want every devout mind to OBSERVE THE POWER OF THE HOLY SPIRIT AS DEVELOPED IN STEPHEN'S DEATH, IN ORDER THAT WE MAY LEARN TO RELY UPON THAT POWER.

Here our grapes hang in clusters, and we would have you note them one by one. I would have you observe, first, that although Stephen was surrounded by bitter enemies, no doubt railing and caviling, and muttering their observations to disturb him and distract his mind, yet *his defense is wonderfully logical, clear, consecutive, and forcible.* If you read the seventh chapter through, you might think it was delivered from this pulpit to an audience as affectionate, appreciating, and attentive as you may be: it does not read like an address delivered to a furious mob of bigots, gnashing their teeth at the lone, brave man. In calm, cool, deliberate, bold, stinging language, he deals with them fearlessly and without reserve. He takes the sharp knife of the Word and rips up the sins of the people, laying open the inward parts of their hearts, and the secrets of their souls: between the joints and the marrow he deliberately inserts the two-edged sword, and discovers the thoughts and intents of their hearts. He could not have delivered that searching address with greater fearlessness had he been assured that they would thank him for the operation; the fact that his death was certain had no other effect upon him than to make him yet more zealous. What secret spirit helped him thus to speak? Had he prepared that speech with long elaboration and forethought? Had that oration been carefully composed, revised, and learned by heart? Far from it. He was not so unmindful of our Savior's words. "But when they deliver you up, take no thought how or what ye shall speak: for it shall be given you in that same hour what ye shall speak. For it is not ye that speak, but the Spirit of your Father which speaketh in you." Seized upon, doubtless, without previous notice, and dragged before the council without being allowed a moment for deliberation, Stephen stood up and defended himself, and the truth as it is in Jesus, with all the skill of a practiced debater, with all the deliberation of one laboriously prepared, and with all the vigor of one whose zeal was like a fire in his bones. To what do we trace this mouth and wisdom, which his enemies could not gainsay? To what, indeed, but to the Holy Spirit? The Holy Spirit exerts such a power over the human mind, that when it is His will, He can enable His servants to collect their scattered thoughts, to concentrate all their powers upon one topic, and to speak the words of truth and soberness with unwonted power. Moreover, the Lord can also touch the stammering tongue, and make it as eloquent as the tongue of Esaias of old, to proclaim the truth in the name of the Lord. I will not argue, my brethren, that a minister, when called to speak for Christ, ought at all times to speak extemporaneously. I am so far removed from that opinion that I conscientiously believe that when we have the opportunity for studying the Word, if we waste it in idleness, it is mere presumption to trust to the immediate inspiration of the moment; but I will say as much as this, that if the Christian minister, or if any one of you be called to speak for your Master when you can have had no preparation, you may confidently depend upon the Spirit of God to help you in your hour of difficulty—ay, and I will go farther, and that if more of our ministers believed in the power of the Spirit of God to help them in their preaching, their preaching would be more effective, and God would own it more greatly to the conversion of souls. It seems to me a curious piece of absurdity, if not a specimen of blasphemy, for a preacher to ask the help of the Holy Spirit in his preaching, and then to pull his manuscript out of his pocket. Where is the room for the Holy Spirit to work? Have they not bolted and barred the door against Him? What thoughts can He suggest? What emotions can He excite? The paper is the guide of the hour. Why, then, should they mock the Holy Spirit by asking for His assistance—an assistance which they will not follow? Or, if I shall have committed every word to memory, and prepared every sentence, and then shall come into the pulpit and ask to have an anointing from the Holy One to help me to speak, what do I but ask

Him to do what I do not want Him to do, since I can do quite as well without Him as with Him, and should be thrown out of my course if He did assist me. It seems to me that, after due study of the Word, if the preacher—if you, dear friend, the teacher—will cast yourself upon the teaching of the Spirit of God, though distractions may occur, though in the congregation or in the Sunday school class there may be much to throw you off your track, and to make you lose the thread of your discourse, if you can rest upon the Spirit of God, He will enable you to speak with power, point, propriety, and personality. It is better to be taught of the Holy Spirit than to learn eloquence from the rules of oratory, or at the feet of masters of rhetoric. The Spirit of God needs to be honored in the church in this respect. I am quite sure that if He were more glorified we should find more who spoke with power, because we should find more who spoke with the Holy Spirit. Let this first remark stand with you for what it is worth, and I am persuaded that there is far more in it than some will care to see.

Notice next, *the energy of the Holy Spirit conspicuously displayed in the manner and bearing of the martyr.* What a right royal and triumphant bearing the man has! He does not stand in the midst of the raging multitude with his eyes fixed upon the ground as though, humbly patient, and doggedly resigned, he felt crushed and overwhelmed; neither does he cast his eyes around to observe a gap in the dense ring of cruel persecutors; he has no wish to elude the penalty of witness-bearing. He gazes steadfastly up into heaven. They may gnash their teeth, but they cannot disturb that settled gaze. Their noise and vehemence may roar like the raging waves of the sea; but from the serene depth of his inward peace, his soul looks upward to the eternal throne, and is ravished with unutterable delight. He despises the tumult of the people, not because he is contemptuous toward *them*, but because his whole soul is swallowed up in blissful adoration of his God. He looks up to heaven, and what he beholds through its opened portals makes him careless of the bloodthirsty foes below. Wondrous picture! Behold the man of shining countenance steadfastly looking up, as though he tracked the road through which his soul would soon wing its way; as though he saw the angelic bands ascending and descending to minister to him; as though he held perpetual and abiding fellowship with the great Father of spirits, and was not to be disturbed or distracted by the rage of men. The bearing of many of the martyrs has been singularly heroic. You will be struck in reading "Foxe's Acts and Monuments," to find how many of the humblest men and women acted as if they were of noblest blood. In every age the line of martyrs has been a line of true nobility. When the King of France told Bernard Palissy that, if he did not change his sentiments, he should be compelled to surrender him to the Inquisition, the brave potter said to the king, "You say I shall be compelled, and yet you are a king; but I, though only a poor potter, cannot be compelled to do other than I think to be right." Surely the potter was more royal than the king. The cases are numberless, and should be as household words among you, in which humble men, feeble women, and little children have shown a heroism which chivalry could not equal. The Spirit of God has taken the wise in their own craftiness, and answered the learned out of the mouths of babes. The answers of uneducated persons among the martyrs were frequently so pat to the point, and hit the nail so well on the head that you might almost suppose they had been composed by an assembly of divines; they came from a better source, for they were given by the Holy Spirit. The bearing of the bleeding witnesses for our Lord has been worthy of their office, and right well have they earned the title of "The *noble* army of martyrs." Now, my brethren, if you and I desire to walk among the sons of men without pride, but yet with a bearing that is worthy of our calling and adoption as princes of the blood royal of heaven, we must be trained by the Holy Spirit. Those men who are cowardly, whose profession of religion is so timid that you scarce know whether they have made it or not; those men who go cap-in-hand to the world, asking leave to live, know nothing of the Holy Spirit. But when the Holy Spirit dwells in a man, he knows the right and holds the right, and is not the servant of men. Humblest among the humble in all things else, when it comes to a matter of conscience he owns no master but his Master who is in heaven. No child of God need fear the face of the great, for He is greater than they; He is God's true aristocrat: God has put within Him a spirit of uprightness and sternness for the right which the world cannot bend, let its blasts howl as they will. I pray God we may learn the manliness of Christianity, for much injury has been done to the faith by professors adopting another mode of procedure, and fawning and cringing before the mighty. That upward glance seems to say to us: "Eyes up, Christian! eyes up; let your heart go up to heaven; let the desires mount; let the whole soul fly toward heaven." With heaven in our eye, we may walk through the crowds of men as a lion walks through a flock of sheep, and our fellowmen shall involuntarily own our power.

The power of the Spirit was also very conspicuously seen in the case of Stephen in another respect, namely, in *the calm and happy spirit which he manifested*. I see no fear, I mark no sign of trepidation; he wipes no hot sweat from his brow; he faints not, much less does he offer any plea by which he may escape from their cruel hands. He never walked out of that gate of Jerusalem with a more joyous and tranquil spirit, on the brightest day of summer, than on that occasion when they dragged him out to die— still, resigned, calm, and happy. It is a great thing for a Christian to keep himself quiet within when turmoil rules without. When the mind gets distracted, we are not able to judge of what is wise. A disturbed and distracted spirit generally rushes in foolish haste to escape from the difficulty, and falls into sin in some form or other. To be calm 'mid the bewildering cry, confident of victory; to be still and know that God is God; to stand still with the children of Israel at the Red Sea and see the salvation of God; this is hard, so hard that only the divine dove, the Comforter, can bring us from above the power to be so; but when once the art of being still is fully learned, what strength and bliss is in it! How many of us in the face of death could return death's stony gaze? If it were now decreed that at this moment you must lay down your life, could you smile? Why, the mere thought of it disturbs you, but the fact would alarm you beyond degree. But not so Stephen, his soul rests at anchor in an unruffled haven. Oh! it is in these solemn test moments, when we are not merely talking of death and vain gloriously boasting of our love to Christ, but when death actually comes, and our love is sternly put to the trial, it is then that the omnipotence of the Holy Spirit is seen, when He gives to His servants that sweet peace which none can know but the man who enjoys it.

I have not yet declared all the glorious works of the Holy Spirit upon this first Christian martyr: in addition to the accuracy of his defense, and the royalty of his manner, and the happiness of his spirit, the Spirit of God was even more clearly seen in *his holy and forgiving temper.* In his dying prayer he imitates his Lord: "Lay not this sin to their charge." He stood erect when he prayed for himself, and I know not that he spoke aloud; but when it came to praying for the multitude around him, his spirit acquired a greater vehemence and earnestness. We are told in the first place, that he knelt down, as if to make them see how he prayed, and then he prayed with a loud voice, that they might hear as well as see; he spent his last expiring breath in a loud cry to heaven, that his murder might not be laid at the door of his persecutors. O sweet Spirit of the Son of man lingering still on earth! "Father, forgive them, for they know not what they do," has been the pattern and the forerunner of ten thousand prayers of a similar heavenly character. It has been the mark of a Christian to die patiently, with forgiveness on his lips. Thousands of those who wear the ruby crown this day, and are

> Foremost of the sons of light,
> 'Midst the bright ones doubly bright,

passed away from earth with just those very words upon their lips. Surely, this is a work of the Holy Spirit indeed! We can scarce forgive those who offend us but a little; we find it not altogether easy to *live* at peace with all men, but to *die* at peace with them, and to die at peace with our murderers, what shall I say of it? Surely, this is what the world cannot understand— a celestial, a divine virtue, which must be implanted in human hearts by God himself.

Note once more, the power of the Spirit was seen in enabling Stephen, at such a juncture, when the stones were rattling about his ears, and his body was bruised and mangled by them, *to pray one of the most prevalent prayers that ever went up to heaven.* The prayer we have just mentioned did not die in the air outside Jerusalem's gate; it passed through the gate of pearl, it reached the heart of God, and it obtained an answer. See that eager, impetuous, young man yonder, about thirty years of age. The clothes of the witnesses are laid down at his feet; he desires to have a prominent part in stoning the hated Nazarene; he is one of the most fiery of those ferocious bigots; he belongs to the synagogue of Cilicia, and, having been defeated in argument, he rejoices that harder weapons are at hand; he is glad to see the heretic die; he gloats his eyes with the spectacle, for he feels that Moses, and the law, and the rabbis, and the traditions, are this day avenged. Mark that young man well, for Stephen's prayer is meant for him, though he knows it not. It may be that he heard the plaintive petition and despised it. It is just possible that having heard it, he went away to sneer at it, and to remark upon the hypocritical character of those disciples of Jesus who could lisp their leader's dying words as if they were their own. Yet I think that blessed petition must have rankled in his heart; he must have felt that there was a spirit there far better than his own. Whether or not that prayer remained with him just then, in after years he must have looked upon Stephen as being, if anyone was, his spiritual father, by whose dying prayer he was begotten unto God. In speaking of his conversion, surely Paul must have thought within himself it was the prayer of Stephen that was the means of changing Saul the persecutor into Paul the apostle of the crucified Son of God. Ah! well, my friends, you and I cannot always prevail in prayer, even in sunshiny weather, but what a grand Spirit must that be who could help Stephen thus to unlock heaven's gates in the dreary article of death; to have power with God; to pluck the Savior by the sleeve, and to bring him to save this guilty, raving persecutor, just when the stones were falling upon him, and his flesh was being batted and bruised. O blessed Spirit, though the outward man decays, you renew the inner man day by day.

Behold, beloved, how independent of outward circumstances the Holy Spirit can make the Christian! See what a bright light may shine within us when it is all dark without! See how firm, how happy, how calm, how peaceful we may be when the world shakes to and fro, and the pillars of the earth are removed! See how even death itself with all its terrible influences, has no power to suspend the music of a Christian's heart, but rather makes that music become more sweet, more clear, more heavenly, until the last kind act which death can do is to let the earthly strain melt into the heavenly chorus, the temporal joy into the eternal bliss! Let us have confidence, then, in the blessed Spirit. Are you looking forward, my dear friend, to poverty? Does your business decline? Do you see clearly before you that you will have to put up with the woes of penury? Fear not; the divine Spirit can give you, in your want, a greater plenty than the rich have in their abundance. You know not what joys may be stored up for you in the cottage which grace will make the cottage of content. Are you conscious of a growing failure of your bodily powers? Do you expect to suffer long nights of languishing and days of pain? Oh, be not sad! That bed may become a throne to you. You little know how every pang that shoots through your body may be a refining fire to consume your dross—a beam of glory to light up the secret parts of your soul. Are the eyes failing? Do you expect blindness? Jesus will be your light. Do the ears fail you? Do you hear but few sounds? Jesus' name will be your soul's best music, and His person your dear delight. Socrates used to say this—"Philosophers can be happy without music"; and we Christians can be happier than philosophers when all outward causes of rejoicing are withdrawn. In You, my God, my heart shall triumph, come what may of ills without! By Your power, O blessed Spirit, my heart shall be exceeding glad, even should all things fail me here below.

May this first point be practically serviceable to you! Trust the Holy Spirit: rely firmly upon Him, and He will not suffer you to be confounded.

The Source of Stephen's Dying Comfort

THE SOURCE OF RICHEST COMFORT WILL NEXT BE INDICATED, WITH THE HOPE THAT WE MAY LEARN TO LOOK THERE.

It was the end and aim of the Holy Spirit to make Stephen happy. How could this be done? By revealing to him the living and reigning Savior at the right hand of God. Whether or not Stephen saw literally with his eyes the Lord Jesus standing at the right hand of God, we do not know. It is possible that what is meant here is that his faith became so unusually strong that he had the most clear and vivid sense of Christ's reigning in heaven, so much so that it might be fitly said that he actually saw the Lord Jesus standing at the right hand of God. If it were really a supernatural vision, you and I have no ground to expect a repetition of it, but, if it were a vision of faith, as I think it was, there is no reason why we should not enjoy it even now. If we have like precious faith with Stephen, since it is a great fact that Christ is there, there is no reason why our faith should not see what Stephen's faith saw, and this day our soul's eyes may see Jesus, and our souls may receive the same joy and gladness out of a sight of Christ which Stephen obtained therefrom.

What then did Stephen see? He saw first, that *Jesus was alive*. This is no small thing.

> He lives, the great Redeemer lives—
> What joy the blest assurance gives!

Alive, too, after the crucifixion! Stephen knew that Christ had died upon the cross. In that fact was the confidence of his soul; but he saw that, though once dead and buried, Jesus still lived. Herein was great comfort for Stephen: he was not serving a dead Christ; he was not defending the honor of a departed prophet; he was speaking for the Friend who still existed to hear his pleadings, and to accept his testimony. Stephen argued within himself, "If Christ lives after crucifixion, why should not Stephen live, through Christ, after stoning? If the nails of the cross sufficed not to leave the Savior dead, neither shall the stones from the Jews avail to rob Stephen of resurrection. Jesus rises from His grave, and Stephen shall rise also. No mean assurance this. It is a rich source of comfort to you and to me this day, if conscious of our frailty and of the near approach of mortality, because Jesus lives we shall live also.

Moreover, Stephen not only saw Jesus living, but he knew that Jesus saw him and sympathized with him. Is not that the meaning of the attitude which the Lord assumed? We are told that our Lord sits at the right hand of God "expecting till his enemies be made his footstool," and yet in the text He is not seen as sitting, but as standing. Why standing? One of the old fathers says it was as though the Lord Jesus stood up in horror at the deed which was being done; as though He were about to interpose to help His servant die, or to deliver Him out of their hands. He stands up, actively sympathizing with His suffering witness. Well, beloved, this is just what we see in heaven. The Man of sorrows is alive, and sympathizes with His people still. Though raised to the throne of glory, He is not forgetful of our shame and sorrow. Think not, O child of earth, that the Son of man has forgotten what temptation means, and is now a stranger to human weakness and infirmity. "In all your affliction he is afflicted." He deeply sympathizes with every one of His tried brethren, "and in his measure feels afresh what every member bears." Suppose not that He is an unthoughtful, uncaring spectator of your grief. I tell you, child of God, Christ has risen from His throne to succor you. He stands at this moment in the hour of your extremity, ready to help you. He will send you comforts when you need them, and He will see that our strength shall be to your day. What a sight was this for the dying Stephen! Jesus is living, and living with the same love in His heart which He showed on earth, with the same tender sympathy which He manifested among the twelve when He lingered among the sons of men.

The brightest point in the vision was this: he saw *Jesus standing at the right hand of God.* That was the point in dispute. The Jews said the Nazarene was an impostor. "No," said Stephen, "there he is: he stands at the right hand of God." To Stephen's mind the point was settled by what he saw. This was the main thing—the only thing, indeed, that Stephen cared for; he craved to have his Lord exalted, and he saw Him exalted. The people rage, the rulers take counsel together, but yonder is the King upon the holy hill of God; beyond a doubt He is a reigning monarch, and to

Stephen's heart this was all he wished. If any fear had been felt by Stephen, it was not for himself, it was for the church. He thought, "These wolves tear me first: what will become of the rest of the sheep? How will any escape from their fangs?" He looked up, and there stood the Shepherd looking down upon the wolves, and saying to His dearly purchased sheep, "Fear not, little flock; for it is your Father's good pleasure to give you the kingdom." That seems to me to be the grandest part of the vision—Christ living, Christ loving, and Christ reigning, the triumphant Savior, at the right hand of God.

My brethren and sisters, this doctrine has been to my own soul the only one which has cheered me in times of extremely deep depression of spirit. As I have told you before, so I tell you now—I have known what it is to be brought so low in heart that no promise of God's Word gave me a ray of light, nor a single doctrine afforded me a gleam of comfort, and yet, so often as I have come across this text, "Wherefore God also hath highly exalted him, and given him a name which is above every name," I have always found a flood of joy bursting into my soul, for I have said, "Well, it is of no consequence what may become of me if my name be cast out as evil, and if I myself am left in darkness; if pains should multiply; if sorrows should increase beyond number, it does not matter—I will not lift up a finger so long as my Lord Jesus is exalted." I believe that every genuine Christian heart that loves the Savior feels just that. Like the dying soldier in the hour of battle, who is cheered with the thought, "The general is safe; the victory is on our side; my blood is well spent, my life well lost, to win the victory." Let Christ reign, and I will make no bargain with God as to myself. Let Jesus be king the whole world over, I care for nothing else; let Him wear the crown; let the pleasure of the Lord prosper in His hands; let His covenant purposes be fulfilled; let His elect be saved; let the kingdoms of this world become the kingdoms of our Lord and of His Christ, why, what matters it even though ten thousand of us should go pining through the valley of the shadow of death—our lives and deaths were all well spent to earn so great a reward as to see Jesus glorified.

I would like to put this telescope then to the eye of every sorrowing Christian here, because having had so sweet an influence upon my own heart, surely it might comfort theirs. Dear friend, you are troubled this morning, you are cast down, you do not prosper as you could wish in heavenly things; well, but Christ is not troubled, He is not cast down; and the great fight, after all, goes rightly enough; God's great purposes are subserved; Christ is glorified. Here are two or three pearls for you, gaze upon them, and prize them. First, remember that our exalted Savior is exalted to *intercede* for you. If He has power, He uses it in prayer for you. Christ has no merit which He does not plead for you. Jesus has received no reward, in consequence of His death, which He will withhold from you.

Dear to the Father He is, but He uses that influence on your behalf; Joseph said to the butler, "Speak for me when it shall be well with you"; but the butler forgot him. It is well with Jesus today, and, depend upon it, it is well with you also, for the Well-beloved cannot forget you; and as He always has the Father's ear, He will pray the Father for you, and whatsoever you need shall surely be given you. Recollect too, that Christ has this power, not only to intercede for you, but to *prepare a place for you.* Christian, if Christ be a king of boundless wealth, yet He disdains not to use the wealth of His royal treasury to furnish that mansion of yours most richly, so as to make it worthy of the giver who shall bestow it upon you. Moreover, Jesus is in glory as *your representative.* You are virtually in heaven at this very moment in God's esteem. Your representative is there. My head is in heaven, wherefore should I fear? How can God give heaven to the head, and hell to the foot? As sure as Christ is there, everyone of those who are virtually united to Him shall be there also. Only prove that Christ is in heaven, and you have proved that every believer must be there. Christ's body cannot be mangled. You cannot cut the spiritual body of Jesus into pieces, and throw one limb of it into hell, while the head goes up to glory. Because He lives, we shall live also; and it is His will that where He is, there should also His people be. Jesus is in heaven full of power—there to intercede, to represent, to prepare; but that far-reaching power darts its rays down to earth, "The keys of *providence* swing at the girdle of Christ. Believe it, Christian, nothing occurs here without the permit or the decree of your Savior, who loved you and gave Himself for you. Does the enemy rage? Jesus will put a bit between his jaws, and turn him back "Surely the wrath of man shall praise You: the remainder of wrath shalt thou restrain." Your Lord Jesus Christ has all power in heaven and in earth, and all this power He will exert to bring everyone, even the weakest of His children, into His bosom. Blessed be the sweet love of God which has given us an omnipotent Shepherd to watch over us by night and by day! His head is crowned because He has conquered all His foes. Surely, we may see in that crown of victory the indication that no foe shall ever be able to conquer us, I wish that I could bring out to you the sweetness of the thought of Jesus glorified as I have enjoyed it in my own heart; but it does charm me to think sometimes that as surely as sin, death, and hell, are under the feet of the Son of Man, so surely shall these very feet of mine be set upon the dragon's neck. If I am in Christ, as certainly as Jesus is a conqueror, so shall I be more than a conqueror through Him that has loved me. What sweeter sight could Stephen see than this, when the enemy was at his worst, still Christ was unconquered! and Stephen could read in that the fact that Stephen would be unconquered too; the stones that felled and crushed him would not destroy him; the voice of his blood would cry from the ground, and the spiritual Stephen would become the victor over the hosts of error; the truth would spring out of the dust, and blossom like a sweet flower, and God would be glorified when His servant was slain. Thus I have indicated to you the delightful vision which can give us comfort. Lord, open our eyes to see it.

The Effect of This Heavenly Comfort upon Stephen

Finally, THE COMFORT ITSELF is worth a moment's consideration.

We do not find that the appearance of Jesus in the heavens stopped the stones. When the Son of man came into the furnace with Shadrach, Meshach, and Abednego, the fire did not burn the three holy children, but on this occasion, though the Son of man was there, the fire did burn Stephen. Stephen's life is not spared. He dies as certainly as if Jesus had not been there. That is the plan of the present dispensation. The Lord Jesus does not come to us to forbid our suffering, nor to remove our griefs, but He sustains us under them. We beseech the Lord three times that this or that may depart from us; it does not depart—that is not the general way with God—but we get the answer, "My strength is sufficient for thee; my strength shall be perfect in weakness." It was so with Stephen. The stones fell; they beat about his head; they stopped his eloquent tongue; they dashed into his heaving lungs; they bruised his tender heart. There lay his mangled corpse, an object of love and of lamentation to the saints that were at Jerusalem. The love of Christ had not preserved the flesh. And who ought to expect it? We have heard it said, "If Christ died for his people, how is it that *they* die?" Such questioners forget that the people of God must die because Jesus died: the death of the flesh is no ill, but a blessing. It behooves us to tread in the Savior's steps, that we also may die unto the flesh, but be quickened in the Spirit. The death of Stephen we do not look upon as a calamity. The death of the flesh was but a needful fellowship with the crucified Redeemer, for he did not die as to his spirit—that enjoyed immortality which the rugged masses of rock which were heaved upon him could not injure. Stephen's glorious comfort was in being sustained within, though not shielded from without—in being preserved as to his inner man, though the outer man was bruised and battered. This is the comfort you and I may expect. Through the darts we must go, and they must stick in our flesh, but yet they shall not poison the blood of our soul. Beneath the pitiless storm of hail we must stand, and yet no hailstones shall be able to smite our hearts to injure them. Through the furnace we must go, and the smell of fire must pass upon us, but yet we shall come out of the flaming heat uninjured by the blazing fire. 'Tis ours to suffer and yet to conquer, to die and yet to live, to be buried and yet to rise again. How sweetly is Stephen's triumph pictured in those last words, "He fell asleep." This is the life as well as the death of a Christian. When the world has been most in arms against a believer, it is wonderful how God has given to His beloved sleep, how the saint has rested with perfect composure in the sight of his enemies, and his cup has run over in the time of drought. Calmly on the bosom of his God he has laid his head, and left his troubles for his God to bear. This shall be the death of the Christian. Let his death be as painful as that of Stephen, it shall be quite as composed. He shall shut his eyes to earth and open them to heaven. His body shall but sleep in that royal sepulcher where Christ himself once reposed to be awakened by that heavenly trumpeter who shall bring the tidings of resurrection to the sleeping myriads of the saints. Courage, brethren and sisters, because the Holy Spirit dwells in us, and because Christ up yonder is triumphant for us. Let our tribulations abound, our consolations also shall abound by Jesus Christ, and we shall be more than conquerors through Him that has loved us.

I wish you all had a share in these precious things. If you had, it would not matter how badly I spoke of them; they would charm your souls. But if you do not understand them, I pray that you may. May the Spirit of the Lord open your eyes to see the power of the Spirit and the glory of Christ, and may you and I ere long see Him face to face in paradise. Amen.

12

*I Was Before**

Who was before a blasphemer, and a persecutor, and injurious (1 Timothy 1:13).

I am not going to dwell at this time upon the special items of the text as to what Paul was before his conversion, because none of us have been exactly as he was. We have all gone astray like lost sheep, but each one of us has taken a distinct course from all the rest. You might have to describe your transgressions in very different words from those used by the apostle, because yours has been a different form of guilt from his. Paul said of himself that he "was before a blasphemer, and a persecutor, and injurious." Saul of Tarsus was a blasphemer. He does not say that he was an unbeliever and an objector, but he uses a very strong word, though not too strong, and says that he was a blasphemer. He was a downright, thoroughgoing blasphemer, who also caused others to blaspheme. From blasphemy, which is a sin of the lips, Saul proceeded to persecution, which is a sin of the hands. Hating Christ, he hated His people too. He was also injurious, which I think Bengel considers to mean that he was a despiser; that eminent critic says "blasphemy was his sin toward God, persecution was his sin toward the church, and despising was his sin in his own heart." He was injurious—that is, he did all he could to damage the cause of Christ, and thereby injured himself. He kicked against the pricks, and by doing so injured his own conscience. Having sinned thus grievously Paul makes a full record of his guilt in order that he may magnify the grace which saved even the chief of sinners.

Note here, before we come to the special purpose we have in view, that godly men never think or speak lightly of their sins. When they know that they are forgiven, they repent of their iniquities even more heartily than before. They never infer from the freeness of grace, the lightness of sin, but

---

* This sermon is taken from *The Metropolitan Tabernacle Pulpit* and was preached at the Metropolitan Tabernacle, Newington, in 1880.

quite the contrary; and you shall find it as one trait in the character of every true penitent that he is rather inclined to blacken himself than to whitewash his transgressions. He sometimes speaks of himself in terms which others think must be exaggerated, though to him, and indeed to God, they are simply true. You have probably read biographies of John Bunyan in which the biographer says that Bunyan labored under a morbid conscientiousness, and accused himself of a degree of sin of which he was not guilty. Exactly so, in the view of the biographer, but not so in the view of John Bunyan, who, startled into sensitiveness of conscience, could not find words strong enough to express all his reprobation of himself. Job said once, "I abhor myself." That is a very strong expression, but, when he saw his own sin in the presence of God, the man of whom the Lord said unto Satan, "There is none like him in the earth, a perfect and an upright man, one that feareth God, and escheweth evil," the man against whom the devil himself could not bring an accusation, yet says that when he saw God, the brightness of the divine holiness made him so conscious of his sin that he exclaimed, "Now mine eye seeth thee. Wherefore I abhor myself, and repent in dust and ashes." Those who have seen the exceeding sinfulness of sin by the light of the Holy Spirit, and who have been made truly penitent, are the last persons to speak lightly of evil. They dwell upon their own criminality with many terms to set forth how greatly they have felt it.

We will consider the case of Paul just a minute or two, because it is a type and pattern of the work of God's grace in other believers. He tells us in the sixteenth verse of this chapter, "For this cause I obtained mercy, that in me first Jesus Christ might shew forth all long-suffering, for a pattern to them which should hereafter believe on him to life everlasting." He was a model convert, a typical instance of divine long-suffering, a pattern and specimen of all who believe on Christ, and all conversions are to a large extent similar to that which transformed the blaspheming, persecuting, despising Saul of Tarsus into the great apostle of the Gentiles. Now, notice when he is describing his own past life how he dwells upon it with painful minuteness. He is not speaking before God in private, as Job was in the words we have quoted, else I can conceive that he would paint his sin in still darker colors; but he is answering for himself before King Agrippa touching the things of which he had been accused by the Jews, and you will see that he puts his offense against Christ and His church in as strong a light as he very well could. His enemies have no such accusation to bring against him as that which he voluntarily makes against himself.

First, he says in the tenth verse of the twenty-sixth chapter of the Acts of the Apostles, which we read just now, "Many of the saints did I shut up in prison." Those whom he shut up in prison were saints. To imprison the guilty were no fault, but to maltreat and shut up holy men was indeed blameworthy. He confessed that they were saints, saintly persons, but he

committed them to prison for that very reason, because they were
Christians; and therefore their saintly lives did not protect them from his
malice, but made them so much the more objects of his cruel hatred. He
says that he hunted the saints; and not merely a few of them, but "Many of
the saints did I shut up in prison." He lays stress upon the word
"many"—not half-a-dozen here and there, but scores and hundreds suffered
through him and his persecuting band. He crowded the prisons with the followers of Jesus Christ. "He that toucheth you toucheth the apple of his
eye," says the Lord of hosts when addressing captive Zion. One touch of
a saint of God injuriously given will be painful to the Lord; how much
more, then, when there are many such touches, and when he whose hand
has done the evil deed has to confess—"Many of the saints did I shut up
in prison." We may be quite sure that he did this because they were
Christians, for the ninth verse puts it thus, "I verily thought with myself that
I ought to do many things contrary to the name of Jesus of Nazareth." It
was Jesus of Nazareth he was aiming at, though his blows were directed
against his followers. It was because the name of Jesus was named upon
these people that they were put in prison. Now, this is no small sin—to persecute holy men, to imprison many of them, and to do so simply
because they believed in Jesus Christ. The apostle felt that this put exceeding bitterness into the gall of his transgression: that he had lifted up unholy
hands against the members of Christ's body, and through them had wound-
ed their ever-glorious Head. More than this, he did not merely put them in
prison, but he says, "Many of the saints did I shut up in prison." Some persons in prison have had a measure of liberty, as Joseph had, but Saul took
care that these believers should be straitly shut up, that they should have
no liberty. He put them into the common jails, locked them up, and made
their feet fast in the stocks, causing them to suffer even as he and his companion Silas afterward did in the prison at Philippi.

Continuing the summary of his evil-doings against the servants of the
Lord, he says, "I was not content with their imprisonment, but I was eager
for their death. When they were put to death, I gave my voice against them;
when the Sanhedrim wanted a vote I, young Saul, was there to give my
maiden vote against Stephen or any other saint. If the chief priests wanted a knife to cut the Christians' throats with, there was I ready to do the
deed; if they needed one who would drag them away to prison and to
death, there stood I, the eager messenger, only too glad if I might lay hands
upon them, believing that I was thereby doing God service." "Nay," says
he; "that is not all. I punished them oft in every synagogue, and compelled
them to blaspheme." This, indeed, was a very horrible part of Saul's sinfulness. To destroy their bodies was bad enough, but to destroy their souls
too—to compel them to blaspheme, to speak evil of that name which they
confessed to be their joy and their hope, surely that was the worst form that

even persecution could assume. He forced them under torture to abjure the Christ whom their hearts loved. As it were he was not content to kill them, but he must damn them too. "I compelled them to blaspheme." This was a dreadful sin, and Paul mentions it as such. He does not extenuate his crime, nor attempt to find excuses for his conduct; and then he adds, once more, that he did all this wickedness with the greatest possible enthusiasm: "And being exceedingly mad against them," like a raging madman in his fits, like a violent maniac, who cannot be held in—seized with frenzy, tearing right and left, finding no rest unless he could be harrying and worrying the sheep like a bloody wolf, as he was to the sheep of Christ's flock— "being exceedingly mad against them, I persecuted them even unto strange cities." He scattered them far and wide, and then sought to get authority that even when they were in exile they might not be beyond His reach. Saul seems to have grown proficient in the science of persecution, and to have become a very master in the cruel art of crushing the people of God.

We do not learn this from James, or John, or any of the other apostles. Who tells us of all this? Who makes out this long, black catalogue of crimes of which the man who committed them might well be ashamed? Why, Paul himself. It is Paul himself that puts it so; and I would that, in like manner, the worst character you could have, my brother, might come from your own lips. "Let another praise thee, and not thine own mouth; a stranger, and not thine own lips"; but, when there is an accusation that must be made against you, be you the first to make it with tears of repentance before the living God.

I think I have thus, from the example of Paul before Agrippa, justified the expression with which I started, that true penitents do not seek to extenuate or diminish the sin which has been forgiven them, but they own how great it is, and set it forth in all its enormity as it appears before their enlightened eyes.

Now, I want you, dear friends, who know the Lord, to follow me in a very simple way, rather by your emotions than by anything else. I want the text of my sermon to be, "I was." The apostle tells us what he was—what he was before conversion. Now, I want you to think what you were before the grace of God met with you, and changed you. I do not know that I shall help you much to recollect the details of your sin, for almost the last time I stood here I did that when we spoke of Peter from the words—"When he thought thereon, he wept"; but I want you to see seven very profitable inferences which will arise out of an impartial retrospect of your life before conversion.

Adoring Gratitude

The first, I think, will be that IF WE THINK OF WHAT WE WERE IT WILL EXCITE IN US ADORING GRATITUDE.

Paul was full of gratitude, for he thanked Christ Jesus that he counted
him faithful, putting him into the ministry. He is so glad of the favor of
God that when he comes to the seventeenth verse he must put down his pen
while he sings, "Now unto the King eternal, immortal, invisible, the only
wise God, be honor and glory forever and ever. Amen." If, then, you and
I look back upon what we were before the Lord saved us, we too shall be
full of adoring gratitude as we think of even the least of all the favors that
He has bestowed upon us. "I am not worthy," said the patriarch Jacob,
when he was returning to his country at the command of God—"I am not
worthy of the least of all the mercies, and of all the truth, which thou hast
shewed unto thy servant," and we can each one say the same. Is it not a
wonderful thing that you who were—I will not say what, you know what
you were, and God knows—that you should be a teacher of others; that you
should be permitted to stand up and speak of pardon bought with blood;
that you should be allowed to talk of holiness though your lips used to
speak of any other theme but that; that you should be allowed to extol the
Christ for whom you had no words of praise a little while ago, for whom,
indeed, you had only words of contempt and scorn? Paul was astonished
to think that he was put into the ministry; when I look back upon my own
life before I knew the Lord, I am amazed that ever I should stand here, seeing that for so long I refused my Lord's love, and put aside His favors, and
would have none of them. Ah, I did not know what would happen to me
one day. Little did I then think that I should ever stand here to—

> Tell to sinners round,
> What a dear Savior I have found.

But it does fill me with gratitude which makes me bow before God in
thankful adoration to think that He should have looked on me, and to know
that "unto me," as well as unto Paul, "is this grace given, that I should
preach among the Gentiles the unsearchable riches of Christ."

I ask you, dear friends, to recollect this gratitude in the reception of
every blessing. When you enjoy church privileges, when you come to the
communion table, think, "Here comes one to sit with the children of God
who once was like a dog outside the house." When you stand up and praise
the Lord, think, "And I too am permitted to offer the sacrifice of
praise—I, who once sang the praises of Bacchus or of Venus, rather than
of Christ Jesus!" When you draw near to God in prayer, and know that He
hears you too—when you have power in prayer, and prevail with the Most
High, and come back with your hands full of blessings that have been
obtained at the throne of grace, you may well say, "What shameful things
these hands once did when I rendered my members instruments of unrighteousness; and now they are loaded down with the bounties of a gracious
God!" Oh, do bless His name! If you do not, the stones in the street will

begin to cry out against some of you. Oh, if your heart does not leap at the very sound of the name of Jesus, surely you cannot possess a heart at all. Such a change, such a wondrous, matchless change, has passed upon you that if you do not praise the Lord today, and tomorrow, and as long as you have any being, what shall be said of your ungrateful silence? "I was"—I was before—all that I ought not to have been, but grace has changed me, and unto the God of grace be all the glory. Do not all of you who love the Lord unite with me in this utterance of adoring gratitude?

Deep Humility

A second very blessed inference (we can only speak briefly upon each one) is that A SENSE OF WHAT WE WERE SHOULD SUSTAIN IN US VERY DEEP HUMILITY.

It did so in the case of the apostle Paul; and I would refer you to his expression of it in the first epistle to the Corinthians, the fifteenth chapter, and the ninth verse, where he says, "I am the least of the apostles, that am not meet to be called an apostle, because I persecuted the church of God." When he was compelled to glory in what he was through the grace given unto him he said that he supposed he was not a whit behind the very chiefest apostles; yet he here says of himself that he was not worthy to be called an apostle, because before his conversion he persecuted the saints of God. Now, dear brothers and sisters, if we have been a little while converted, and have united with the church of God, and the Lord has given us a little work to do, we may be tempted to think, "Now, I am somebody. Really, I am not now quite the humble dependent that I used to be; I am getting to be of some service to my Lord and Master, and I am of some importance in His church." Ah, that is the way many Christians get into sad mischief. "Pride goeth before destruction, and a haughty spirit before a fall." You must always strive against that kind of spirit, and one way to avoid it is to remember what you were in your unregenerate state. There are some who might say, "I am a minister of the gospel, but I am not worthy to be called a minister, because of the sin that I committed before my conversion. I am a member of the church of Christ, but I am scarcely worthy to be called a member; because I was before a blasphemer, or a Sabbath-breaker, or profane, unchaste, or dishonest." Recollect what you were, and let your spiritual advancements never lead you to unspiritual pride and self-conceit, for "every one that is proud in heart is an abomination to the Lord."

I have heard of a good man in Germany who used to rescue poor, destitute boys from the streets, and he always had them photographed in their rags and filth just as he found them; and then in years afterward, when they were clothed and washed and educated, and their characters began to develop, if they grew proud he would show them what they were, and try to teach them what they would have been likely to be if it had not been for his charity. If you are inclined to lift up your head, and boast what a great man you are now, just look at the likeness of what you were before the Lord made you a new creature in Christ Jesus. Oh, who can tell what that likeness would have been but for the interpositions of divine grace? I think you would say what the Scotchman said to Rowland Hill when he called to see the good man in his study. He sat and looked at him, and Rowland Hill's face, you know, if you have seen his portrait, is one to be remembered; there is a peculiar comic look about it. So the Scotchman said, in answer to the question, "What are you looking at?" "I have been studying the lines of your face." "And what do you make out of them?" said Mr. Hill. "Why, that if the grace of God had not made you a Christian, you would have been one of the worst fellows that ever lived." "Ah!" said Mr. Hill, "and you have hit the mark this time." I should not wonder too, if some of us, when we look in the glass, were to see somebody there that would have been a very deep-dyed sinner if it had not been for the change of heart which sovereign grace has wrought. This ought to keep us very humble, and very lowly before God. I invite you, friends, to think this over, and when you feel yourselves beginning to swell a little, let the bladder of your foolish and wicked pride be picked with the needle of conscience as you recollect what you used to be, and you will be all the better for letting some of the gas escape. Come back as speedily as you can to your true shape, for what are you, after all? If you are anything that is good, or right, or pleasing in the eyes of the Lord, still you must say, "By the grace of God I am what I am."

> All that I *was*, my sin, my guilt,
> My death, was all mine own;
> All that I *am*, I owe to thee,
> My gracious God, alone.
>
> The evil of my former state
> Was mine, and only mine:
> The good in which I now rejoice
> Is thine, and only thine.

Well, those are two of the inferences which result from looking back at what you were; the retrospect excites gratitude and sustains humility.

Genuine Repentance

The next is this—THE REMEMBRANCE OF OUR FORMER CONDITION SHOULD RENEW IN US GENUINE REPENTANCE.

When we look back upon what we used to be before the Lord met with us, it should breed in us a perpetual repentance. There are some who seem to think that we only repent of sin when we are first converted. Do not you be deluded by any such false notion. When you leave off repenting, you have left off living. You are not living to God as you ought to do unless you daily repent. Remember, that we are not saved by a single act of faith which terminates the moment we receive the assurance of the divine forgiveness, but by a faith which continues as long as we live, and as long as ever we have any faith we must have repentance too, for these are twin graces—faith with a bright eye, like Rachel, who was beautiful and well-favored, and repentance, tender-eyed, like Leah, but with a lovely eye for all that. "Repentance," says one, "why, I thought that was a bitter thing that was taken away when we believed!" No, but it is a sweet thing; I could wish to repent in heaven; though I suppose I shall not. We cannot carry the tear of penitence in our eye into heaven; it will be the only thing we might regret to leave behind. Surely we shall be sorry even there for having grieved our God. Even there, I think, we shall repent, but certainly as long as we are here we must daily repent of sin—ay, and repent of the sin that is forgiven, repent more because it is forgiven than we did when we had any doubt about its being pardoned.

> My sins, my sins, my Savior!
> How sad on thee they fall,
> Seen through thy gentle patience,
> I tenfold feel them all.
>
> I know they are forgiven,
> But still their pain to me
> Is all the grief and anguish
> They laid, my Lord, on thee.

Smite on your breasts while you think that it was necessary that Christ should die that you might be delivered from sin, and its penalty and power, and as your love increases let your sorrow abound, that such a Lord should have needed to be crucified for you. Oh, sin, as Christ becomes more lovely, you become more hateful, and as our soul learns more of the beauty of holiness, it perceives more of your ugliness, and so continually loathes you more and more. If you want to draw up the sluices of repentance, sit down and remember what you were by nature, and would have remained if grace had not intervened. So, then, it shall be good for you to say, "I was before a blasphemer, and a persecutor, and injurious," or to use any other expression that shall accurately describe you, if it lead you, like Peter, to go out and weep bitterly true tears of repentance.

Fervent Love

And now, fourthly (we have but a word on each inference, you see), THE RETROSPECT OF OUR PAST LIVES SHOULD KINDLE IN US FERVENT LOVE to the Lord who has redeemed us.

You remember Christ went into the house of one of the Pharisees who had a measure of respect for Him: this was Simon, who desired Him to eat with him; but when He entered in, Simon treated Him as a common guest, and offered Him none of the delicate attentions who men give to choice friends, or to superiors. Christ took no note of this, nor had He need to do so, for there was another who stole into that room who did for Him all that Simon ought to have done, and more than Simon could have done. "A woman in the city, which was a sinner, when she knew that Jesus sat at meat in the Pharisee's house, brought an alabaster box of ointment, and stood at his feet behind him weeping." She stood behind the couch upon which He was reclining, and let her tears fall down upon His blessed flesh till she had washed His feet with them, and then unbraiding the luxurious tresses of her hair, she wiped those holy feet with it; her love, her humility, her adoration, her penitence mingling as she kissed His feet, and anointed them with the ointment which she had brought. Our Lord explained why this woman had performed this extraordinary action. He said it was because she had been forgiven much. Now, rest assured that this is a rule without an exception, that those who are conscious of having had much forgiven are those who will love Christ much. I do not say—I almost wish I could—that love is always in proportion to the amount of sin forgiven; but I do say that it is in proportion to the consciousness of sin forgiven. A man may be a less sinner than another, but he may be more conscious of his sin, and he will be the man who will love Christ most. Oh, do not forget what you were, lest you should become unmindful of your obligation to Jesus. You are saints now, but you were not always so. You can talk to others of Christ now, but you could not once have done it. You can wrestle with the angel in prayer and prevail now, but once you were more familiar with the devil than you were with the angel. At this moment your heart bears witness to the indwelling of the Holy Spirit: it is not long ago that the prince of the power of the air wrought within you, and the Holy Spirit was not there at all. I beseech you, therefore, forget not this, lest you forget to love Him who has wrought this wondrous change in you. I think there is nothing better than to retain a vivid sense of conversion in order to retain a vivid sense of love. Do not be afraid of loving Christ too much. I see the cold carping criticism of this age objects to any expressions of love to Christ which we use in our hymns because it says that they are sensuous. My only answer to such talk is—God give us more of such blessed sensuousness! I think that instead of diminishing these utterances it will be a token of growth in grace when they are more abundant, not if they become so common as to be hypocritical; then they would be sickening; but as long as they are true and honest, I for one would say to you who love the Lord, go on and sing—

Safe in the arms of Jesus,
Safe on his gentle breast.

Go on and sing—

Jesus, I love thy charming name,
'Tis music to mine ear.

Hesitate not to say—

Thou dear Redeemer, dying lamb,
We love to hear of thee;

and if it shall please you, and the Spirit shall move you, even say, like the spouse in the song, "Let him kiss me with the kisses of his mouth: for thy love is better than wine." The starveling religion of the present day, not content with tearing away the doctrinal flesh from the spiritual body, is now seeking to drag out the very heart of religion, and to reduce Christian experience to nothing but a chilly doubting of everything. Let this be far from you. Believe something, and love something, for to believe is to live, but to love is to be in health. Oh for more love arising out of a deep, intense sense of what we once were, and of the change which Christ has wrought in us! "But," says one, "I do not know that any great change has been wrought in me." No, and there are some who tell us that we do not want any. There are certain Paedo-baptists preaching nowadays that the most of children of pious parents do not need conversion. We have long had the Church of England teaching us baptismal regeneration; now we have got some Nonconformists trying to persuade us that no regeneration at all is wanted. This a new kind of doctrine that I know nothing of, and that the Word of God knows nothing of, and it will not do for us. It will eat out the very life of Christianity if it be believed. Pious ancestors could not save one of you—even if your fathers and mothers, and grandfathers and grandmothers, and great-grandfathers and great-grandmothers, and great-great-great-great-grandfathers and great-great-great-great grandmothers, as far back as ever you like, had been all saints, nevertheless, their faith could not avail for you. You must be born, "not of blood, nor of the will of the flesh, nor of the will of man, but of God." "Ye must be born again" is as true of one child as of another; as true of you as it was of me, and as true of me as of the thief confined in prison today. But some of us have been changed, we are washed, we are sanctified, we are justified in the name of the Lord Jesus and by the Spirit of our God. It has been a real work of grace, the turning of us upside down, the reversing of the course of nature, a turning of night into day, a turning of the powers of our spirit from the dominion of Satan to the dominion of Christ; and we must and will therefore love Him who has wrought in us such a wondrous transformation.

Ardent Zeal

Well now, fifthly, REMEMBERING WHAT WE WERE, ARDENT ZEAL SHOULD
BE AROUSED IN US.

Look at Paul. He says "I was before a blasphemer, and a persecutor, and
injurious." What then? Why, now that he has become a follower of Christ,
he cannot do too much. He put many saints in prison: now he goes into
many prisons himself. He hunted them even to strange cities: and now he
goes into all manner of strange cities himself. He dragged them before tri-
bunals and now he himself goes and stands before Roman proconsuls, and
before the Roman emperor himself. Paul can never do too much for Christ,
because he has done so much for the devil. I remember one who lived four
or five miles away from a place of worship, who used to say, "You old
legs, it is no use being tired; for you have got to carry me. You used to take
me to the place of amusement when I served the devil, and you shall carry
me now to the house of God that I may worship and serve Him." When
sometimes he had an uneasy seat, he used to say, "It is no use grumbling,
old bones, you will have to sit here, or else you will have to stand. Years
ago you put up with all kinds of inconveniences when I went to the theater,
or some other evil place, when I served Satan; and you must be content to
do the same now for a better Master, and a nobler service." I think some
of us might take a lesson from that old man, and say to ourselves, "Come,
covetousness, you are not going to hinder me from serving the Lord. I used
to be liberal to the devil, and I do not intend now to be stingy to God." If
ever I am tempted in that fashion, I will give twice as much as I had
thought of doing, so as to spite the devil, for he shall not have his way with
me. Some, when they serve Satan, go as if they rode a racehorse, and whip
and spur to get in first. How they will destroy body and soul in the service
of the evil one; but if a Christian man gets a little lively they say, "Oh, dear
me, dear me, he is excited, he is fanatical, he has grown enthusiastic." Why
should he not be in earnest? The devil's servants are enthusiastic; and why
should not the servants of Christ be the same? Black prince, black prince,
are you served by heroes, and shall Christ be served by dolts? Oh, let it not
be so, my brethren. Surely if anything can wake up all the powers of our
nature, if anything can make a lame man leap as a hart, if anything can
make a palpitating, trembling heart to be bold and brave for Christ, it
should be the love which Christ has shown in looking upon such as we
were, and changing us by His grace. "Ah, but you must not do too much,"
says one. Did you ever know anybody who did? If anybody ever does too
much for Christ, let us rail off a piece in the cemetery that we may bury
him in it. That grave will never be wanted, it will be empty until Christ
comes, "Ah, but you may have too many irons in the fire." It depends upon
the size of the fire. Get your fire well hot—I mean get your heart well hot,
and your nature in a blaze; then put all the irons you can ever get into it.

Keep them all at a white heat if possible. Blow away, and let the flames be very vehement. Oh, to live for God a life of ecstatic zeal even if it were only for a short space of time. It were better than to have a hundred years of bare existence, in which one went crawling along like a snail, leaving slime behind, and nothing else. It were better far than driveling out, as oftentimes we do—

> Our souls can neither fly nor go
> To reach eternal joys.

The love of Christ to us, then, suggests great zeal in his service.

Hopeful About Other People

Now, sixthly, I am sure that another inference that should be drawn from it is this: If we remember what we were, and how grace has changed US, IT OUGHT TO MAKE US VERY HOPEFUL ABOUT OTHER PEOPLE. Paul was, for he says, "This is a faithful saying, and worthy of all acceptation, that Christ Jesus came into the world to save sinners; of whom I am chief. Howbeit for this cause I obtained mercy, that in me first Jesus Christ might shew forth all long-suffering, for a pattern to them which should hereafter believe on him to life everlasting." Well, friend, you are saved: then anybody can be. You never ought to despair of the salvation of anyone, for you know yourself, and feel yourself to have been the most undeserving of men; and yet God's grace has really made you to love Him. Well, then, that grace can light on anybody. Already it has fallen on the most unlikely spot possible. Now, from this moment never indulge the idea that it is useless to attempt to benefit any of your fellowmen. I recollect—indeed, I have often met with the circumstance of persons saying, "Why did you not ask So-and-so to attend a place of worship?" "Ask him? Oh, I never thought of him." "Why not?" "I did not think it was any use." It is a very singular thing that those are the kind of people who, if you do get them to hear the word, are generally converted—the people you think it is no use to bring. Men who have been accustomed to speak very disrespectfully of religious things when once brought under the sound of the truth are often the first to receive a blessing. Those are the kind of fellows to try at, for there is some hope of reaching men who are in such need of the gospel we have to proclaim as they are. You know there is virgin soil there, so it is the very place to sow the good seed of the kingdom. There is good fishing in a pond that never was fished in before: and here is a man who at any rate is not gospel-hardened: he has not got used to the sound of the word, so as to take no notice of anything that is said. Bring him in; he is the very man we want: bring him in. "But he is a swearer." Well, but if you were a swearer before your conversion, you ought never to say anything about that. "Oh, but he is a very hardened man." Yes; but if you were converted, notwithstanding what you were, you ought never to make that objection against anyone. "Oh, but he is such a low-bred man." Well, there are plenty of us who cannot boast much about our aristocratic descent. "Oh, but," says one, "he is such a proud man, such a haughty man"; or, "he is a rich man; he is a purse-proud man." Yes, but there are others like him who have been brought in; and while that man has sinned in one way you have sinned in another way; and if the grace of God met your six it can meet his half-dozen. Depend upon it, God meant us to be hopeful about other people when He saved us. See that man coming out of the hospital. He has had pretty nearly all the diseases you ever heard of, and yet he has been cured. He is not the man to say, "It is no use going in there, you will get no good by putting yourself under the treatment of that doctor": on the contrary, whenever he meets with anybody who is suffering, he says, "You go and try the physician that healed me. If you can get a bed under his care, if you can come under his notice, you are almost certain to get cured, your maladies cannot be worse than mine, and he met my case exactly, and he can meet yours." He is the man who will advertise Christ, and will proclaim His fame the whole world over—who has tasted that He is gracious, and has proved in his own case the converting power of the Holy Spirit. Oh, I pray you, dear friend, despair of nobody. You who go with your tracts, go into the worst houses; you who talk in the workhouses to those who are, perhaps, as far gone as any—who find them dying in the infirmary, and rejecting the word as you speak it, yet keep on; keep on. "Never say die" concerning any. Since the Lord has saved you the grace of God can save anybody, however far he may have sunk in sin; it can reach even to the very vilest of the sons of men.

Confidence for Ourselves

The last inference is, that WHAT GOD HAS DONE FOR US SHOULD CONFIRM OUR CONFIDENCE FOR OURSELVES—our confidence, not in our selves, but in God, who will perfect that which He has begun in us. There is not half as much grace necessary to bring you to heaven if you are a believer as you have had already to bring you where you are. You have got to be perfected; but remember that it was the very first step that had the difficulty in it. It always reminds me of the legend of St. Denis, who picked up his head after it was cut off, and walked, I think forty leagues with it. But a wit said that there was no trouble about walking forty leagues: the difficulty all lay in the first step. So it did; and so all the difficulty of the walk of faith lies in the first step—that first coming of a dead heart into life, that first bringing of a reprobate soul, a carnal mind that is enmity against God, into friendship with God. Well, that has been done; that first great work has been wrought in by God the Holy Spirit; and now you can say with the apostle, "If, when we were enemies, we were reconciled to God by the death of his

Son, much more, being reconciled, we shall be saved by his life." Do you think the Lord ever converts a man with a view of showing him the light that he may go back again into the thick darkness forever? Does He drop a spark of heavenly light into our souls that it may go never to be rekindled? Does He come and teach us to eat heavenly bread, and drink the water of life, and then leave us to starvation or die of thirst? Does He make us members of Christ's body, and then allow us to rot and decay? Has He brought us thus far to put us to shame? Has He given me a heart that cries after Him, and pines for Him; has He given me a sighing after perfection, an inward hunger after everything that is holy and true; and does He mean, after all, to desert me? It cannot be—

> His love in time past forbids me to think
> He'll leave me at last in trouble to sink;
> That gracious conversion I have in review,
> Confirms his good pleasure to help me quite through.

So let us go on our way rejoicing that it shall be even so with each of us. Amen.